EASY-TO-MAKE
BIRD FEEDERS FOR WOODWORKERS

by
Scott D. Campbell

DOVER PUBLICATIONS, INC., NEW YORK

Easy-to-Make Bird Feeders for Woodworkers is a new work,
first published by Dover Publications, Inc., in 1989.

Manufactured in the United States of America
Dover Publications, Inc.
31 East 2nd Street
Mineola, N.Y. 11501

Library of Congress Cataloging-in-Publication Data

Campbell, Scott D.
Easy-to-make bird feeders for woodworkers.

Bibliography: p.
1. Birdhouses—Design and construction. 2. Woodwork.
I. Title
QL676.5.C275   1989   690'.89   88-30926
ISBN 0-486-25847-5

CONTENTS

LIST OF TABLES

ACKNOWLEDGMENTS

Special thanks to those individuals, agencies, associations, and companies who gave unstintingly of their time, freely sharing information from their special areas of expertise, and without whose kind help this book would surely have suffered. More specifically:

Thanks to Frank Dunkle, Director, and Bill Knapp of the U.S. Fish and Wildlife Service for their help in obtaining a copy of *Special Scientific Report—Wildlife No. 233*. Never in all the years that I have dealt with government agencies has a response been so efficient.

Thanks to William T. Robinson, President, and Edward L. Keith, P.E., Senior Engineer, of the American Plywood Association for their detailed and informative response to inquiries about plywood products and for permission to reprint the Association's registered trademark.

Thanks to James S. Hill, President, and Dwight M. Brown of Geo. W. Hill & Co., Inc., a large regional supplier of wild-bird seed and wholesale distributor of commercial bird feeders to retail outlets, who extended themselves in every way possible to make the information contained herein both thorough and complete.

Thanks to Tim Williams, Manager/Naturalist, of the Clyde E. Buckley Wildlife Sanctuary, the oldest National Audubon Society sanctuary in the central United States, for sharing information on his own extensive bird-feeding experience.

Thanks to Jonathan Burpee, Director, Customer Relations, of W. Atlee Burpee Company for helpful information on the Aviarium™ manufactured by The Aviarium, Inc., South Yarmouth, Massachusetts.

INTRODUCTION

Just how popular is bird feeding? Surveys indicate that as many as one-fifth of all households purchase wild-bird seed and that more than 60 million Americans feed birds.[1] In some regions of the country as many as one in every three households may engage in some type of feeding program.[2]

Why has bird feeding become so popular? First, no other wildlife-enhancing activity brings such immediate results. In a matter of days after feeding begins, wild birds are drawn to the feeding stations with rapidly increasing frequency. Second, it is completely democratic. There are no age limits, income levels, or educational requirements. Within the limits of his or her own resources each person determines individually what food is selected, how much, and how it is presented. Third, it is one of the few options available to the layman to directly affect the course of wildlife management. Few people can actually afford to operate their own wildlife preserve. With a carefully planned and well-executed feeding program, however, each farm or suburban yard—even a tiny apartment terrace—can become a mini wildlife sanctuary. Collectively such efforts have even helped some bird populations to expand into new territories. The Evening Grosbeak's eastward expansion in the late nineteenth and the twentieth century, just to cite one example, is credited to the increased planting of box-elder trees and the proliferation of sunflower-seed feeders. Finally, and perhaps most important, it's just plain fun for the whole family. Together, parent and child alike discover the wonders and diversity of the bird world.

---

[1] Aelred D. Geis and Donald B. Hyde, Jr., *Wild Bird Feeding Preferences: A Guide to the Most Attractive Bird Foods* (Washington, D.C.: National Wildlife Federation, 1983), p. 1.

[2] Aelred D. Geis, *Relative Attractiveness of Different Foods at Wild Bird Feeders*, Special Scientific Report—Wildlife No. 233 (Washington, D.C.: U.S. Dept. of the Interior, Fish and Wildlife Service, 1980), p. 1.

Secretive species attracted in no other way to your view suddenly become exciting discoveries enjoyed much as they must have been experienced for the first time by early explorers in the New World. There are exotic colors to see, from the palest blue to the most dazzling crimson, a seemingly endless multitude of avian melodies to serenade you on life's daily journeys, and delightful antics to enliven even the drabbest winter day.

For the woodworking enthusiast who is also a bird lover this means double pleasure. There is both art and skill in taking a blank piece of timber and shaping it to the mind's-eye vision of what it should become. To create an object pleasant in form and beauty is rewarding in itself but to produce what is both useful and clearly appreciated as well is the ultimate high.

This does not mean that there are not some excellent commercial feeders, and, indeed, the amateur would do well to learn from them, but most commercial offerings suffer from a number of unfortunate compromises. To begin with, most feeders are manufactured far from their point of sale. To keep down shipping costs this means the use of many lightweight and typically short-lived components. Plastics, for instance, tend to crack and fade or discolor after extended sun exposure. Higher-quality glass is virtually eliminated not only because of its weight but also because of its potential fragility in long-distance freighting. Style and selection are also limited because the large-scale manufacturer finds it more economical to produce fewer components and to target the broadest segment of the market. For this reason seed hoppers tend to be small (perhaps also in keeping with packaging and freight requirements) and follow the same basic styles—lantern, barn, tube, and the two-sided cabin or chalet style.

Yet, you, the reader, as woodworker or wildlife enthusiast, have access to a veritable infinity of possible styles, sizes, and special features limited only by your own imagination. To assist this creativity the following pages will explore various design considerations, construction techniques, seed preferences, and general attraction tips. Actual designs using a variety of materials and balanced for all skill levels are also included.

Whatever your interest—commercial production for a local crafts fair, club or father-son projects, or simply personal relaxation and enjoyment—it is hoped that this book will be your guide to many hours of pleasurable productivity.

I. Construction Basics

Construction Materials

There are two basic components of most bird-feeder designs: a seed hopper with one or more transparent plastic or glass sides, and the supporting structure, including roof, floor, and usually one or more sides, which are typically, though not always, nontransparent. As plastic and glass will be discussed in depth in a later section of this chapter, it is the supporting structure with which we are now concerned.

Wood, as you have no doubt already surmised from the title of this book, is the preeminent material of choice for bird-feeder construction. Its selection is obvious for a number of reasons, including availability, durability, wide range of sizes, moldability (through sawing, drilling, bending, planing or shaping, sanding, and joining), and finishing versatility (involving multiple techniques with or without numerous paints, stains, and sealers).

Commercially, wood is available through a wide range of dealers, from the full-line lumber companies selling virtually every wood product commonly used in the building trades, to the less specialized "home improvement centers," which offer fewer options but are more price conscious, with favorable savings to their nonbusiness accounts. Hardware and discount stores may also offer limited selections.

There are two basic considerations when choosing a dealer. First and foremost, as alluded to in the preceding paragraph, is pricing. Most old-line lumber companies offer standard, often substantial, discounts for volume purchases from their business customers. While this is a time-honored and perfectly acceptable position from their standpoint, it sometimes leads to nondiscount prices for individuals which are inflated at best and at times bordering on exorbitant. This is not true in every case or with every dealer in a given locality, and, as the competition from other wood vendors increases, the situation is likely to improve, but do shop around before you buy. Second, many stores act independently of one another in their purchasing decisions and stocking policies—even among some local affiliates of national chains. Some overly zealous salesperson may try to sell you what they have instead of what you want. Once again the message is "Shop around!" Just because store A sells only prefinished redwood shelves and planters and store B seems never to have even heard of redwood, it does not mean that store C does not stock that special redwood siding you seek for your projects.

Millwork is an option limited almost exclusively to full-line lumber dealers and together with selection is one of the two great advantages they have over less specialized stores. Of course millwork also adds to cost and should only be contemplated if full-scale commercial production of nonstandard-size parts is required or a particular design requires sawing, shaping, or other molding operations not readily available in the layman's own shop or workplace.

Perhaps the greatest lesson is that, whenever possible, feeders should be crafted from standard wood sizes to avoid either millwork or unnecessary construction steps. There are two types of lumber most commonly used in feeder construction. These are *dimension lumber*, which is from two inches to just under five inches in thickness and two or more inches in width, and *boards* or *commons*, which are less than two inches in nominal thickness and one inch or more wide.

Both dimension lumber and boards come in standard lengths of 8, 10, 12, 14, and 16 feet, with some longer lengths occasionally available in two-foot increments. (Stud-grade two-by-fours may also be offered in 92⅝-inch, 93-inch, or 94½-inch sizes. Yes, it can get confusing. If you don't specify the length you want you may find yourself buying a shorter size than expected. Also, home-improvement centers sometimes offer shorter board lengths in "pick-your-own" bins or "odd-size" racks though at higher per-board-foot prices.) Boards are further classified from Common #1 to Common #5, with the lowest numbers representing the highest quality—fewer defects such as knots, checks, splits, or shakes.

Practically speaking, "#2" is usually the highest grade available, excluding various nearly blemish-free "select" grades used in furniture making. Fortunately the usually desired rustic appearance of feeders as well as standard exterior-rated finishing techniques permits and at times even demands the use of cheaper grades of board.

The woodworker's world would be much simpler if he could stop here when choosing lumber. Regrettably, he cannot, for both boards and dimension lumber are sized by width and thickness according to the next highest or rounded-off inch of their "green lumber" or fresh-cut size. Since moisture makes up 50 percent of the total weight of some woods[3] and air drying or seasoning alone can result in moisture losses of 12–18 percent[4] it is clear that some shrinkage must occur. Of course lumber is also "dressed," or planed to a smooth finish. For example, a standard two-by-four (so called from its supposed size in inches) typically was cut green as 1$\frac{9}{16}$ by 3$\frac{9}{16}$ inches and dried and finished to an actual size of 1½ by 3½ inches. To the uninitiated the terminology "two-by-four" (2″ × 4″) should mean "two inches by four inches," but clearly this is not so. Table 1 indicates the actual measurements for a wide range of commonly available sizes of both boards and dimension lumber. When planning your own designs you will find yourself referring to it often until you have become familiar with the differences.

Thinner thicknesses and random lengths can also be found in shop lumber or the previously mentioned select grades and "finish" or "cabinet" grades. Sizes such as ⅛, ¼, ⅜, and ½ inch are available and are often sold by craft suppliers by the square foot. Generally they are too thin or too expensive to warrant consideration in most feeder designs.

Thankfully there is one wood product useful to bird-feeder construction which is not sized so ambiguously. It is the ever-versatile *plywood* made from alternating layers, or plies, of thin wood veneer positioned at right angles to adjoining pieces for added strength. Usually available in 4-by-8-foot panels, or sheets, it can sometimes also be found in 2-by-2-foot sizes for smaller projects. The range of thicknesses seems almost endless. Plugged and touch-

---

[3]James J. Hammond and others, *Woodworking Technology* (Bloomington, Illinois: McKnight & McKnight Publishing Company, 1961), p. 19.
[4]*Ibid.*, p. 23.

TABLE 1
Lumber Sizes[5]

Type	Nominal Size (The purchase size—designation in inches)	Actual Dressed Size (in inches)
Board lumber	1 × 2	¾ × 1½
	1 × 3	¾ × 2½
	1 × 4	¾ × 3½
	1 × 5	¾ × 4½
	1 × 6	¾ × 5½
	1 × 8	¾ × 7¼
	1 × 10	¾ × 9¼
	1 × 12	¾ × 11¼
Dimension lumber	2 × 2	1½ × 1½
	2 × 3	1½ × 2½
	2 × 4	1½ × 3½
	4 × 4	3½ × 3½

sanded panels intended primarily for floor underlayment come in
$^{19}\!/_{32}$-, $\frac{5}{8}$-, $^{23}\!/_{32}$-, $\frac{3}{4}$-, and 1⅛-inch sizes. Fully sanded panels come in
$^{11}\!/_{32}$-, $\frac{3}{8}$-, $^{15}\!/_{32}$-, $\frac{1}{2}$-, $^{19}\!/_{32}$-, $\frac{5}{8}$-, $^{23}\!/_{32}$-, $\frac{3}{4}$-, $\frac{7}{8}$-, 1-, and 1⅛-inch sizes. The
303® siding panels are commonly available in $^{11}\!/_{32}$-, $\frac{3}{8}$-, $\frac{1}{2}$-, $^{19}\!/_{32}$-, and
$\frac{5}{8}$-inch sizes.[6] Naturally, locally stocked sizes depend upon demand
and not all sizes will be available in all localities or at all times.

Conveniently, each sheet of plywood is stenciled either on one side
(Figure 1) or along the panel edge with a "strip stamp" for the very
highest grades. These trademark stamps give various data on how
and where the panel was made. Only three items are of particular
relevance in bird-feeder construction. They are: (1) *Interior vs. exterior.*
Exterior-rated plywood is made with waterproof glue and selected
veneers for greater durability in moist conditions. Most interior-
rated plywood is also made with waterproof glue now but the quality
of the veneers may be much poorer. Clearly "exterior" is superior for

[5]*Lowe's 1974 Buyers Guide* (North Wilkesboro, N.C.: Lowe's Companies, Inc., 1974), p.
11.

[6]Edward L. Keith, P.E., Senior Engineer for the Technical Services Division of the
American Plywood Association, personal communication with author, 8 September
1987.

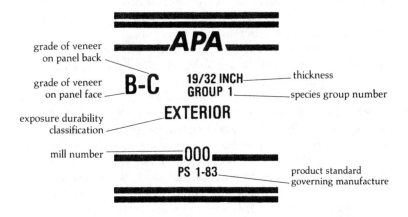

Fig. 1. Plywood trademark stamp (courtesy of American Plywood Association).

outdoor applications but on occasion "interior" may suffice if cut edges and sides are carefully sealed with a high-quality paint. Do not take "exterior" to mean invincible, however. All plywoods require some protection with either paints or stains in exterior applications. (2) *Thickness.* Designated in fractions of an inch, the thickness of plywood used in bird-feeder construction should in general be no less than ½ inch. Thinner plywoods using fewer plies are more susceptible to warping or surface cracks as the finish ages. This does not mean that they cannot be used in some limited applications, but they will require more care. (3) *Veneer grade* or finish quality as designated by hyphenated capital letters. Both sides of a plywood panel are graded with a letter rating from "A" to "D." "A" is highest quality. "D" allows for knots and knotholes up to 2½ or sometimes 3 inches wide. Even "A" grade allows for plugs or repairs of minor defects but the patches are neatly made and do not affect overall quality. For most feeder applications "B–C"-graded plywood is sufficient. Naturally the best, or "B," side is turned outward in construction (usually, *though not always,* the trademark stencil is placed on the lowest-veneer-grade side).

Other commercial products to consider for limited applications are the various siding products (made of plywood or hardboard in rough-sawn, V-groove, lap, barnboard, or other styles). Because they are factory finished, however, they may require special edge treatments to protect and disguise edge cuts in more complicated feeder designs. Wood shingles, or shakes, may also be used for interesting effects. Hardwood dowels in three-foot lengths and a wide variety of diameters including ⅛, ³⁄₁₆, ¼, ⁵⁄₁₆, ⅜, ⁷⁄₁₆, ½, ⅝, ¾, and 1 inch are extremely useful for perches and other specialized applications. "Hardware cloth," which isn't really cloth at all, is a galvanized wire fencing product that is sometimes used, particularly in the construction of suet holders. Available in three-foot heights and several mesh sizes, it is sold in rolls of ten, twenty-five, or fifty feet and frequently can be purchased by the foot. Both dowels and hardware cloth are found at most lumber-supply dealerships, home-improvement centers, hardware stores, and craft shops.

Many unconventional sources of lumber are also available with much of the supply free or at nominal cost. Shipping pallets, or skids, raised wooden platforms used to store and transport freight, are routinely discarded by trucking companies, warehouses, and large factories. It simply isn't worth the high labor cost to repair them when nails give or boards break and their value has long since been depreciated on the company books. Construction sites often have refuse piles for random lengths of wood, and full-service lumber dealers may have millwork discard bins. Labor and storage costs are the culprit here. It isn't cost-effective to store odd, short sizes of wood until a use can be found for them. Barn or building remodeling or demolitions also offer opportunities, as do old furniture parts and shelving at garage and yard sales. Sawmill waste, driftwood, and logs from storm-downed trees (aged at least six months and preferably longer for dimensional stability) make rustic and quite attractive feeders.

Scavenger hunts can be fun and more than just thrifty. There is a special satisfaction in restoring a long abused and neglected wood to its natural beauty and function. To make your search a happy and successful one as well, a few tips should be kept in mind. (1) *Not all seeming refuse is actually discarded.* A few companies, still in the minority, recycle waste for boiler fires in their heating plants or sell it to outside vendors. It is only common courtesy to ask before you take and could save potential embarrassment. (2) *Pay attention to names.* Everyone likes to be remembered and it will save time to know whom to contact if questions arise. If you plan to visit often, a thank-you card or an inexpensive gift might be in order (reception-ists are always losing pencils and pens, for instance). (3) *If you can't see it, don't bother to ask.* Insurance regulations alone prohibit companies from allowing John Q. Public to roam about their facilities. Nor should they be expected to pay their employee an hourly wage while he escorts you. Fortunately, the popularity of containerized collec-tion systems means that most scrap-lumber drops are outside and easily accessible. (4) *Leave it as you found it.* If wood is neatly stacked be sure it is returned to that condition after you have made your selections. It doesn't hurt to do a little extra. You may find yourself being invited back again. (5) *Expect some surprises.* This is particularly true with shipping containers and skids. Chosen for strength and function rather than beauty or symmetry, individual boards may be rough-sawn and of random width and thickness. If you have the right equipment you may shape and finish any board to your requirements. More often than not, however, you will find it more practical to alter your design (see "Fourplex Cavity Feeder," Chapter IV, for a design made from pallet lumber).

Tools of the Trade

Tool selection is largely a function of personal philosophy. Some individuals prefer power tools for their speed and labor-saving benefits. Others favor a more intimate and personal contact with their work. Although all the designs in this book were crafted with the hand-tool enthusiast in mind, they are equally adaptable for power-tool use.

The required tools can be as basic as a hammer, ruler, and crosscut saw. With a little ingenuity they will handle a wide variety of construction needs. Other aids will simplify labor and make more intricate fabrication strategies a reality. A child's inexpensive plastic protractor, for example, is useful for measuring angle cuts, as is a T bevel. A try square is extremely helpful for drawing straight, or "true," lines, as is a coping or keyhole saw for those special interior cuts and large-diameter holes that are occasionally required by some designs. A brace and bit with a selection of bits for narrow-width holes is most useful for inserting perches or dowels or for pilot holes for nails. (Pilot holes may on occasion require a drill bit as small as $\frac{1}{16}$

inch, too small for braces, so a small bradawl can come in handy if an electric drill is unavailable or unacceptable, but most dowels needed are in the range of $\frac{3}{16}$ to $\frac{1}{4}$ inch.) The backsaw is a personal favorite for those difficult angle cuts because of its short length and more rigid blade that does not flex under stress. C clamps of at least one and preferably two, three, or even four inches in size are indispensable around the average workshop and practically mandatory for some angle or specialty cuts requiring a saw guide for proper alignment (a minimum of two clamps is usually required).

Less often used but occasionally helpful are tin snips or sheet-metal shears (a hacksaw blade taped at one end as a handle will sometimes suffice), a standard screwdriver for mounting hardware, an inexpensive compass for scribing circles (coasters, jar lids, and bottle caps also work), and a small selection of chisels and gouges for scoring grooves or channels for glass inserts or to trim excess wood from logs and timbers.

Among power tools, an electric drill and circular saw are fundamental. Variable-speed, portable jigsaws with adjustable bevel guides can make a wide variety of freehand or specialty cuts. A router is excellent for cutting the grooves required for glass installation and is a real luxury to own.

But should you choose power tools, please remember that any power tool can be both friend and foe—a wonderful time saver or a terrible weapon. Never let children use them without adequate supervision, and always use eye and hearing protectors. (Yes, they can be uncomfortable. It's hard to believe some of the designers actually wore their creations under normal working conditions, but they are important.) Don't underestimate childish curiosity either. Even the most disciplined child can sometimes fall victim to it. Remember how you once emulated your parents and wanted to use "grown-up" tools? Be sure to lock up, temporarily disable, or cut power supplies of all power tools when left unattended if there is any danger of misuse.

Working with Plastics

Having previously condemned plastics for their faults, we must now admit that they have four valuable advantages: namely, light weight, resistance to breakage, transparency (allowing seed levels to be observed), and workability—plastics can be sawn, drilled, routed, cemented, or scored and snap-cut like glass.

Acrylic is the generic name for the thermoplastic material most often marketed under trade names like Lucite®, Acrylite®, and Plexiglas®. Available in sheets of various thicknesses, textures, and colors, as well as clear, it can be ordered cut-to-size from dealers listed under "Plastics" in the yellow pages of your phone book or from some glass dealers. Home-improvement centers and some hardware and discount stores offer a limited selection of precut sizes. For feeder applications the plastic need be no more than ⅛ inch thick (plastic is often sold by gauge size, with larger numbers representing heavier thicknesses).

Acrylic sheets come with a protective paper or film to guard against scratches (a major problem). This coating should be left in place as long as possible during the various fabrication stages to insure a clean, scratch-free finish.

For hand-cutting, mark the paper or use a grease pencil on unmasked stock and score firmly with a knife (inexpensive tools especially designed for this purpose are available wherever glass cutters are sold, or a sharp, sturdy-bladed pocket or utility knife will do). Snap-cutting does not allow for corner cuts. A cut must be made the entire length or width of the panel—whichever requires the least amount of excess material—before the second cut is attempted. After scoring, place the cut line face up on the edge of a firm, smooth surface such as a workbench, and lightly but firmly clamp the straight edge of a board at the inside edge of the cut line. Evenly spacing handholds along the projecting section, apply a sharp downward motion to complete the break. Should there appear to be too much resistance, the cut was not scored deeply enough and must be redone. (See Fig. 3, page 14). A sharp coping-saw blade (15T) works well, but both sides of the cut line should be clamped or held firmly in place to keep the up-and-down motion of the saw from twisting the plastic and consequently forming cracks or fault lines. Twisting will become less noticeable as the cut deepens. For fine detailing and intricate cuts an inexpensive and expendable layer of thin hardboard can be clamped to the acrylic sheet as reinforcement. The saw blade can be allowed to cut directly into this backing without harm.

Power cutting is also possible. Metal-cutting blades are recommended with almost any saw, including radial-arm, band, and table saws. Stationary or portable jigsaws also may be used. Once again, edges of the cut may have to be clamped or held in place with push sticks or scrap lumber securely fastened to the work station to keep them from riding up with the motion of the blade. (*Never place hands near any moving blade!*) Cut edges can be finished with a cabinet scraper or light sanding if desired. The highest finish can be achieved by buffing with an electric polishing wheel, but this is a superfluous operation for most feeder applications.

There is one potential problem with power cutting that should be noted here. If the cutting blade rotates too rapidly, friction may cause the plastic to overheat and gum up the cut. This author has actually cut through an entire piece of plastic only to find that it has completely resealed, albeit imperfectly, behind the cut, leaving the panel weakened but intact. To overcome this, slower saw speeds should be employed, or a spacer can be inserted behind the cutting blade as it progresses to keep the separated edges well apart.

Working with Glass

Although glass is heavier and much more susceptible to breakage than plastic, it is far superior to plastic for most feeder uses because of its excellent scratch resistance and durability. Like plastic, it is available in a number of types and thicknesses, but simple window glass is ordinarily used. Available as $\frac{1}{16}$-inch single-strength window glass or as the better quality $\frac{1}{8}$-inch double-strength (the preferred thickness), it is readily found in cut-to-order size from traditional glass supply outlets. A secondary source is recycled glass found in discarded storm windows or doors. Even cracked or broken glass may have large areas of useable glass which can be cut off from the damaged sections. A word of caution should be interjected here, however. Glass cutting is one of those peculiar, delightfully-simple-appearing operations that require some surprising practice to master. Be prepared to experience a good deal of chipping and breakage before you master the skill. Also, recycled window glass is often securely welded to its frame by many years of paint buildup. If the window is a discard and thus expendable it may be far easier to cut the muntin bars or frame to remove the glass.

Glass is not really cut. It is scored and snapped in a process nearly identical to that for plastic. Begin with a clean sheet of glass. All old paint, glazing compound, and dirt should be removed to prevent

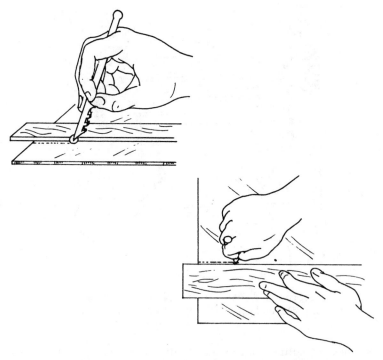

Fig. 2. Scoring glass (note straightedge guide).

interference with the scoring process. Wear gloves and goggles or other eye protection. (Glass does not always break predictably and slivers of glass are wickedly sharp!) Measure and mark the cut with a grease pencil or felt marker. (Cracks in old glass will "run" under pressure into undamaged areas, so be sure to allow plenty of distance between any defects and the scored area.) Place the glass on a clean, flat work surface. Laying a straightedge along the line as a guide, draw the cutter (an inexpensive tool found in most hardware and home-improvement stores) toward you across the pane from edge to edge in one complete motion (Fig. 2). Bear down. A distinct "crackling" sound can be heard as the glass is scored. A well-etched, clearly discernible line caused by light deflection in the scored area should appear as a whitish mark. (If only close inspection reveals the mark, insufficient pressure was applied. Turn over the glass and try again on the reverse side. Drawing the cutting wheel over the same

Fig. 3. Score-and-snap cutting of plastic or glass (always wear gloves and goggles when working with glass).

line dulls the cutter and can shatter the glass.) Next, position the glass with the score line face up and aligned parallel to the very edge of the work table. Clamp a board as a straightedge over the top of the glass parallel to and just meeting the inner edge of the score line. The board should be in firm contact but don't overtighten, or shattering may result. Now, grab the exposed, overhanging glass firmly between evenly spaced, *gloved* hands and pull down sharply with an abrupt, snapping motion (Fig. 3). With experience you may be able to simply raise the pane and rap it down sharply against the table edge without clamping.

In addition to insufficient scoring pressure, some common reasons for failure are stop-and-go scoring, which results in an uneven line; an uneven work surface, causing pressure points or low areas under the glass; and unevenly applied pressure when snapping.

It is usually not advisable to try to score a line closer than ¼ inch from the outside edge of a glass pane. Even then, square-nosed pliers should be used to make the snap. Simple lineman's pliers are sufficient; similar designs with special gripping surfaces for glass are also available. Two pairs may be required for long cuts.

Design Features

The vast majority of feeder designs call for gravity-fed food-dispersal systems. The advantage is that the food is stored and meted out to birds only as they need it. Naturally the food used must be of a relatively uniform size to prevent clogging the dispersal mechanism, sufficiently hard to withstand the crushing weight of compression in a confined area, and comprised of sufficiently small and mobile particles to flow readily without sticking or binding. Fortunately, seeds with their hard shell coating fulfill these requirements admirably. Some hulled products like sunflower chips and, to a lesser extent, peanut hearts also work well although they can absorb moisture and pack together in clumps. Static feeder styles on the other hand—typically, feeding shelves, corn spikes, or suet cakes, logs, or mesh bags—offer all the available food to all comers, usually without any restriction on size or species.

Naturally, for a gravity-fed system to be effective the seed hopper must be relatively higher than it is wide and preferably taper to a narrow base. Wider-base styles can be accommodated if baffles are used to channel the seed to appropriate openings. Exit openings should be sufficiently large to allow for an orderly dispensing of seed but not so large that the seed spills out uncontrollably (see Table 2 for a description of various seeds and their sizes). In most cases the seed opening need be no more than ½ inch high and as wide as the feeder design will allow. If elevated feeding perches are desired at various points, as in typical tube-feeder designs, the seed-opening size becomes more critical. Because of the elongated shape of thistle seed (the primary seed type used in many tube-style feeders) a narrow slit can be made in plastic hoppers, measuring ⅛ inch wide by ¼ inch high (3–4 mm × 7 mm). Most of the seed will stay in the hopper until extracted by the bird. A different approach may be taken with less conveniently shaped seeds. By placing a hood or awninglike shield over the inside of elevated openings, the seed is permitted to flow down around the open, or bottom, edge of the awning just below the entrance hole. Birds are then able to reach into the large access opening afforded by this style and extract seed. In time, as seed is used up, the level will drop below the birds' reach and they will descend to lower perches (see "Five-Position Multiseed Feeder," Chapter IV, for an example of this style). Such features also have the

TABLE 2
Sample Seed Types and Sizing Data

Type	Shape	Color	Size* (length × width × height)
Black-striped sunflower (medium)	elongated	predominantly black with grayish white striping	5/8" × 3/8" × 3/16" 15 mm × 10 mm × 5 mm
Oil (black) sunflower	elongated	black with occasional faint gray striping	3/8" × 1/4" × 3/16" 10 mm × 7 mm × 5 mm
Safflower	elongated	white	5/16" × 3/16" × 3/16" 8 mm × 5 mm × 5 mm
Cracked corn (medium)	irregular	golden yellow and white	3/8" × 3/16" × 1/8" 10 mm × 5 mm × 4 mm
Peanut hearts	irregular	brown	1/4" × 3/16" × 1/8" 7 mm × 5 mm × 4 mm
Sunflower chips (fine)	irregular	grayish white	3/16" × 1/8" × 1/16" 5 mm × 4 mm × 2 mm
Niger (thistle)	elongated	black	1/4" × 1/16" × 1/16" 6–7 mm × 2 mm × 2 mm
White proso millet	spherical	brownish white	1/8" 4 mm

*Size measurements are approximations based on random samples by the author. Seed size can be highly variable depending upon variety, grading, and milling. Check with your dealer for more information on locally available seed types.

benefit of allowing multiple types of seed—either successively or in combination. With larger awning openings it is important to use a coarse screening mechanism of some type which will still leave seed accessible but bar inadvertently luring the feeding bird into the seed hopper, where it will in all likelihood become trapped and possibly panic into aimless efforts to escape.

Seed can spoil, with potentially harmful effects to both birds and pocketbook. Fortunately most seed is consumed too rapidly for serious problems to develop, but some precautions are in order. In hopper-style feeders the hopper should be protected by a roof or cap. (Don't forget to allow for a generously sized fill port with lid or door. Refilling should be a rapid, simple operation involving a minimum of spilled seed or frustration.) In open-style feeders, such as table, or platform, designs, a number of ⅛-inch or larger holes should be drilled to allow for rainwater and snow-melt runoff. Screening can be used over larger holes to keep seed from escaping.

Dirt will accumulate on the glass or acrylic sides of seed hoppers over time. For this reason the interiors should be accessible for cleaning. Accidents do happen. Removable glass inserts not only aid cleaning but also allow quick, painless repair.

Glass stops, which regulate the amount of travel of glass panes in their channels, are a means of insuring adequate spacing between the floor of the feeder and the seed-hopper opening. An obvious technique is simply to regulate the length of the channels, or grooves, in which the glass slides. This calls for careful measurement, however, and not all designs require grooving, since glass can be held in place by cleats or other devices. In some cases, therefore, it may be preferable simply to use a small wooden cleat attached to the floor of the feeder at either side where the glass would normally contact. Since the glass now comes to rest on this narrow strip of wood, a gap is maintained between the glass and floor equal to the thickness, or height, of the cleat.

Suet-restraining wooden pegs or hardware-cloth suet cages are popular additions to the exterior wooden sides of seed-dispensing feeders. Where the use of only one feeder is contemplated this may be preferable but suet is an oily fat which will over time leave stains. It is better to use separate, suet-only designs where possible. Metal, by the way, is no longer considered potentially harmful to perching birds in cold climates—witness the fact that birds can stand on snow or ice for long periods without difficulty.

Perches are another feature almost mandatory in most designs. There are no hard and fast rules here. A ¼-inch hardwood dowel approximately 1½ to 2 inches long and ½ inch below the access hole or seed opening is usually sufficient. Larger birds may be discouraged if desired by thinner diameters set more closely to the walls of the seed hopper.

Seed stops are convenient as well as economical. Small, elevated boards attached to the edges of the feeder opposite the seed openings, they catch seed that otherwise might spill over the side, and they act as informal perches as well. Tube-feeder designs often incorporate a circular disk at the bottom to catch spilled seed, thereby saving waste and reducing seed costs.

A more exotic design feature is the so called "one-way" glass with a highly reflective coating. When feeders so equipped are placed near a window, birds can be observed under nearly natural conditions. Special film coatings can also be applied over existing glass (check with your glass dealer or under "Glass Coating and Tinting" in the yellow pages for local availability). Remember, such coatings are only "one-way" as long as the interior light on the observation side of the feeder is more subdued than that striking the outward or reflective side of the feeder glass. This is easily observed by noting the lighted interiors of many modern, glass-faced office buildings at night, which become invisible in strong daylight.

Partitioned seed hoppers, although primarily novelties, allow more than one type of seed to be used at the same time without mixing. Further, traditional tube feeders force birds to drop to fewer and lower perches as seed levels decline. Compartmentalized feeders where each section is filled separately insure that all perches will be available for approximately the same length of time.

Finally, don't forget seed capacity. Feeders which hold only a quart of seed or less empty rapidly and can become a real chore to refill. Capacity must also be balanced against weight, however, and how and where the feeder will be mounted. Weight shouldn't be a problem for a well-built design of any size but sturdiness isn't much consolation if it bends double or breaks the chosen mounting branch of your favorite ornamental tree or shrub.

Of course, not every available design feature can or should be used in all feeder applications, but these suggestions illustrate the major possibilities.

Squirrel-proofing and Species-specific Designs

If you don't live in an area where squirrels are plentiful you might wonder why anyone would wish to exclude them from feeders. With their charming antics and cute, fluffy tails twitching nervously behind them as they scurry about, they are a delight to watch. Unfortunately, as mammals go, their eating habits are atrocious. They sit astride feeders hogging and hoarding food until none is left for avian visitors or carry food away to be devoured later. Their appetites are prodigious. And if they don't get what they have come to expect, they can gnaw through wood and thin plastic feeders in search of that last elusive seed.

One incident that is particularly illustrative comes to mind. Scraps had been scattered on a window ledge just outside the kitchen window. Though intended for birds, there was both surprise and delight when a gray squirrel appeared one day. It seemed amazing that such a wild creature would venture so close to a human dwelling. One day food was not available at the time the squirrel arrived. Earlier fascination quickly turned to consternation when the squirrel, almost as if in a fit of human pique, began actively gnawing into the muntin bars framing one of the window panes.

Nor are gray squirrels the only culprits. Fox squirrels, flying squirrels, and, yes, even ground squirrels can be a problem. Many ground squirrels are nearly as adept at climbing as their larger cousins. This author has witnessed chipmunks climbing tall trees and daintily traversing utility lines.

How can the squirrels be stopped? That question has been asked by almost every bird lover and feeder designer-craftsman at one time or another. Perhaps surprisingly, the answer is not always the same. Squirrels are intelligent and very ingenious at solving the problem of barriers we try to place in their path. The solution sworn to by one individual may prove completely ineffectual for another. In addition, local conditions such as tall trees near a feeder location may drastically affect the solutions tried from one area to the next in the same region of the country.

In a natural setting, predators would limit squirrel populations and increase the squirrels' wariness of man. Zoning regulations in suburban areas and preservation goals in parks and sanctuaries, as well as the decline of big predators, have led to an unnatural state in which in peak years squirrel populations can explode, often followed by several years of decline. Hunting is impractical and in most cases neither legal nor desirable. Trapping can bring limited, temporary relief, but in the natural order of things population pressures tend to push squirrels ever outward from their place of birth in search of favorable habitats not claimed by others of their kind. All too soon new tenants will inhabit the trees and burrows about your feeding station.

For these reasons the undeclared war against squirrels has shifted to various restricting devices. To best understand what does work it is perhaps instructive to look at what does not. First, squirrels are great leapers (or gliders in the case of flying squirrels). If possible, feeders should be placed no closer than eight feet from trees or utility poles, which might serve as launching platforms (this author has personally measured gray-squirrel leaps of seven and one-half feet). Similarly post-style feeders should in most cases be no less than four feet above ground and five feet is preferred. Metal posts might seem a good solution, but squirrels can grip smaller-diameter pipes with their forepaws as they climb. Metal sheets wrapped around trees or posts (the guards should cover at least three linear feet) discourage cats but not always squirrels as they sometimes grip the overlapping edges of the metal or get a running start and scurry over the surface with a bear-hug-like grip. Hanging feeders also present problems as you might guess if you have ever watched a squirrel tightrope-walk a telephone line or leap the intervening distance between two trees.

What then does work? For post-style feeders a large-diameter support pipe will work but can be expensive, troublesome to install, and aesthetically unpleasing. A compromise involves a small-diameter pipe (e.g., ½ or ¾ inch) topped by a much larger section of pipe six inches or more in diameter and at least twelve inches in height (some authorities recommend three feet). Thus, the venturesome squirrel is denied a running start. He can climb to the larger pipe but then must lean out away from the smaller pole in order to search for a grip to continue his climb—momentum is effectively frustrated. Shields also work well. A round sheet of metal at least twelve inches in diameter with a center mounting hole is slipped over a support pole. There are reports, however, of some squirrels learning to grip and climb over these obstructions. One solution is to use springs or off-center cords to secure the guard from above to allow flexible shifting of the guard when a squirrel applies its weight

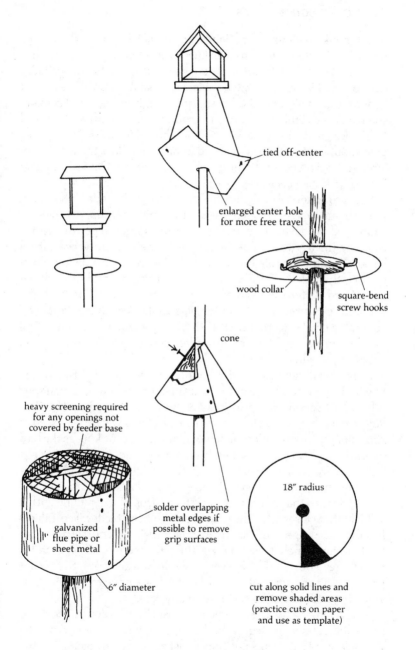

tied off-center

enlarged center hole
for more free travel

wood collar

square-bend
screw hooks

cone

heavy screening required
for any openings not
covered by feeder base

solder overlapping
metal edges if
possible to remove
grip surfaces

galvanized
flue pipe or
sheet metal

6" diameter

18" radius

cut along solid lines and
remove shaded areas
(practice cuts on paper
and use as template)

Fig. 4. Squirrel guards.

in attempts to climb over. Similarly, the shield, or baffle, can be precariously supported from below with what are called square-bend screw hooks ("L"-shaped hooks with a screw tip) or a similar device. The idea is to make the shield so unstable that the slightest added weight will cause it to tip sharply—frightening, if not spilling, the would-be climber back to the ground. (Note: With any squirrel baffle designed to tip, the center hole that slides over the support pole should naturally be oversized in order to allow the maximum amount of travel, or tipping, when activated.) Conical squirrel baffles have also been used with success.

Some commercial designers have used an "over-under" technique whereby a weight hidden inside the primary support pipe is connected to a short section of slightly larger pipe, or sleeve, covering the top portion of the support. When the unwary squirrel tries to climb over this last section of pipe its weight, being much greater than that of the hidden counterweight, pulls the sleeve downward. After the frightened squirrel has released its hold, the counterweight returns the outer pipe to its normal position. The concept is similar to that used with old-style window weights. Still another option is the spring-loaded perch, which drops when excessive weight is added.

A personal favorite is the counterbalanced, weight-activated perch. If you reach back to your memories of the ubiquitous schoolyard seesaw the principle involved is readily apparent. The landing perch is connected via a wire or rod to a weight balanced at some point from the fulcrum, or point of support. As long as the bird or birds alighting on the perch do not exceed a certain weight (adjusted by adding to or moving the weight in relation to the fulcrum) nothing happens. If, however, a large bird or squirrel should disturb that balance, the perch will drop down, pulling with it a shield that closes over the seed opening of the feeder (see Table 3 for various weights of mammals and birds). Of course there are limits to how finely tuned the weight-activated mechanism can be. Sometimes snow, rain, or even heavy dew can "trip" the feeder prematurely and some of the lightest birds are also among the most annoying and cannot be excluded in any case.

As for hanging feeders, protection is usually afforded by a baffle at some point above the feeder on the support wire or, more typically, with a large plastic dome positioned just above and overhanging the feeder. The wide, smooth surface is virtually grip-proof and, when

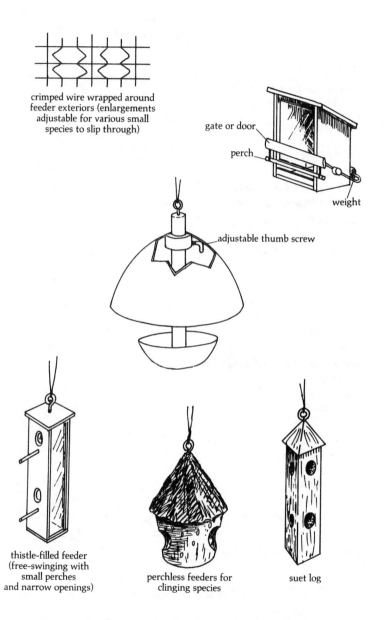

crimped wire wrapped around
feeder exteriors (enlargements
adjustable for various small
species to slip through)

gate or door

perch

weight

adjustable thumb screw

thistle-filled feeder
(free-swinging with
small perches
and narrow openings)

perchless feeders for
clinging species

suet log

Fig. 5. Species-restrictive feeder strategies.

TABLE 3
Weight* Relationships for
Selected Mammals[7] and Birds[8]

Species	Average Weights
Eastern Fox Squirrel (*Sciurus niger*) —the largest tree squirrel	18—38 oz. 510—1075 gm.
Eastern Gray Squirrel (*Sciurus carolinensis*)	15—25 oz. 425—710 gm.
Red Squirrel (*Tamiasciurus hudsonicus*)	5—9 oz. 142—255 gm.
Southern Flying Squirrel (*Glaucomys volans*) —the smallest tree squirrel	1¾—3½ oz. 50—100 gm.
Eastern Chipmunk (*Tamias striatus*)	2¼—5 oz. 66—142 gm.
Common Crow (*Corvus brachyrhynchos*) —males	15½ oz.—1 lb. 6½ oz. 440—638 gm.
—females	14¾ oz.—1 lb. 5½ oz. 419—610 gm.
Common Grackle (*Quiscalus quiscula*)	3—5 oz. 83.5—137 gm.
Red-winged Blackbird (*Agelaius phoeniceus*) —males	2½ oz. 62—65 gm.
—females	1¼—1½ oz. 37—43 gm.
Mourning Dove (*Zenaida macroura*) —males	4⅗ oz. 130 gm.
—females	4⅖ oz. 125 gm.
Blue Jay (*Cyanocitta cristata*)	3 oz. 89.2 gm.
European Starling (*Sturnus vulgaris*)	2¼—3 oz. 64.3—88 gm.

[7]Stanley Klein, *The Encyclopedia of North American Wildlife* (N.Y.: Facts on File, Inc., 1983), see individual species entries.

[8]John K. Terres, *The Audubon Society Encyclopedia of North American Birds* (N.Y.: Alfred A. Knopf, 1980), see individual species entries.

Species	Average Weights
Northern Cardinal (*Cardinalis cardinalis*)	1⅔ oz. 43.76 gm.
Evening Grosbeak (*Hesperiphona vespertina*)	2—2⅓ oz. 52—63.5 gm.
Dark-eyed (Slate-colored) Junco (*Junco hyemalis*)	⅗—1 oz. 16—26.6 gm.
House Finch (*Carpodacus mexicanus*)	¾ oz. 21 gm.
Pine Siskin (*Carduelis pinus*)	⅖ oz. 12 gm.
House Sparrow (*Passer domesticus*)	1 oz. 27 gm.
Carolina Wren (*Thryothorus ludovicianus*)	½—⅔ oz. 14.2—19.7 gm.
Black-capped Chickadee (*Parus atricapillus*)	⅖ oz. 11.8 gm.
Tufted Titmouse (*Parus bicolor*)	¾—⅞ oz. 20.3—25.3 gm.
White-breasted Nuthatch (*Sitta carolinensis*)	⅗ oz. 18 gm.
American Goldfinch (*Carduelis tristis*)	⅖—½ oz. 11.8—13.3 gm.
Song Sparrow (*Melospiza melodia*)	⅗—⅞ oz. 16.4—24.4 gm.

*Avian and animal weights, as with humans, can vary individually. In addition they may vary geographically, seasonally, or by sex. Birds preparing for migration also store energy as subcutaneous fat much as mammals add weight in preparation for winter. Note also that some totals were based on limited samples.

the squirrel alights, the weight overload will tip the shield and its attached feeder to one side, forcing the squirrel to drop to the ground. Some finch feeders also use thistle seed, whereas squirrels favor sunflower seed, peanuts, and corn.

Like squirrels, some birds are less welcome at feeding stations than others because of their large appetites or quarrelsome ways. In addition to the already mentioned weight-restrictive systems there are several options. A common commercial technique is to wrap the perimeter of the feeder in a vinyl-coated wire like that used in garden fencing or flower-bed edging. The mesh can be crimped or expanded to allow smaller birds to reach through while prohibiting access to others. Some birds, like nuthatches, chickadees, and goldfinches, can cling to the sides of a seed opening. Other birds, like starlings and House Sparrows, are less agile and require perches. By eliminating perches or using short, small-diameter sizes positioned close against the body of the feeder, larger or more awkward birds can be discouraged. Hanging feeders, in particular, require more agility because of their free-swinging motion, and some of the larger birds like Mourning Doves or pigeons are forced to seek out more stable feeding platforms. One popular hanging-feeder innovation employs a large-bowl–small-bowl design. The smaller bowl, containing seed, supports a short vertical rod at its center. The large bowl is inverted and attached through its base to this support by a thumb screw or other readily adjustable device. By raising or lowering the inverted bowl, which also acts as an overhead squirrel baffle, the size of the birds that can fly in under it is regulated. As with squirrels, food selection will also have some limiting influence (see Chapter III).

Unconventional Design Materials and Sources of Supply

Having noted in previous sections the wide diversity of materials used in special design features such as the squirrel guard, or baffle, it might seem difficult to find sources of supply close at hand. Yet new design ideas rarely begin with specially prefabricated parts. For example, small-diameter metal pipe for mounting posts can be found in the form of ½- or ¾-inch electrical conduit (sold in ten-foot lengths) as well as similar sizes of steel or copper water pipe. These and still larger sizes of pipe can also be found in plastic (waste- or drain-pipe sizes range from 1½ to 4 inches in diameter). Check at electrical- and plumbing-supply stores or home-improvement centers. (Note: These materials are sold with a variety of fittings that serve to increase their versatility.)

Economically priced bowls, both plastic and wood, for use as large-bird restricters can be found, in the form of salad or serving bowls, at discount and department stores. Aluminum, used for roof valleys or flashing, is also priced inexpensively in 10-foot rolls and widths from 10 to 20 inches at building-supply dealers. Galvanized steel chimney, or flue, pipe is available in 3- to 6-inch-diameter sections 2 feet long—some with a snap-lock feature that allows them to be laid flat until final assembly (sold at home-improvement and many hardware stores). Sheet aluminum for storm-door and other repairs can frequently be found in many discount stores. Some printing processes involve aluminum, and discarded sheets, typically 22 by 30 inches and weighing roughly 12 ounces, are regularly offered for sale in the classified sections of small-town newspapers at nominal prices (painting will probably be required to cover the print image). Galvanized metal is used in heating- and air-conditioning-system ductwork, and discarded major appliances have large areas of pre-enameled sheet metal.

As you can see, many local sources of material, new and used, may avail themselves to the practiced and thoughtful eye. Further, several commercial innovations, particularly the antisquirrel baffles, are sold separately and can simply be incorporated into your own feeder creations as desired.

Construction Tips and Techniques

With any outdoor project the main enemy of lasting durability is moisture penetration. Anything that can be done to prevent or delay its deleterious effects will greatly enhance the life of your creation.

Some woods are much more decay- and weather-resistant than others. Among them are redwood, cedar, and cypress. Even these, however, should be coated with a clear sealer (two coats are advisable), including the edges, before final assembly renders them inaccessible.

Whenever possible, nails and other mechanical fasteners should be galvanized steel, copper, aluminum, or brass. Roof-ridge joints can be covered with thin strips of copper, aluminum, or brass-plated weather strip. (Aluminum soft-drink cans with the logo turned under can also be used, but gloves are necessary during the cutting process, as the thin edges are very sharp.)

As the feeder design allows, nails should be driven perpendicular to the grain of the wood. When nails are driven parallel to the wood fibers, as when driven into the ends of a board, the fibers are wedged apart in a "V-like" fashion. In such cases, withdrawal resistance in softer woods can decline by as much as 25 to 50 percent from that obtained with perpendicular-driven nails.[9]

A lead or pilot hole drilled with a diameter slightly smaller than that of the intended nail reduces wood splitting, particularly in denser woods. Perhaps surprisingly, nails driven with lead holes also have somewhat greater withdrawal resistance than nails driven without such aid.[10]

Stronger bonds between connected parts can also be achieved by the use of various wood-joinery techniques. In addition to their strictly utilitarian functions, wood joints are a sign of the level of skill and craftsmanship of the builder and can be quite attractive in themselves. Wooden cleats or metal brackets can also be used for reinforcement or support, particularly in interior areas where they will not disrupt the overall lines of the design. Further, waterproof glues and mechanical aids such as nails, screws, or corrugated fasteners add to the initial strength afforded by the joint. Glues and sealers or caulks also improve weathertightness. Latex caulks are very versatile in that they come in several colors, are paintable as well, and provide easy cleanup. Silicone sealers rated for exterior use also work well and come in clear or white.

Glass and plastic are best held together with some type of mechanical fastener or devices such as channels or grooves in which they slide for easy adjustment or removal. As mentioned earlier, plastic is readily drilled, and nails or screws can then be used to hold it in place. In some situations only glue or cement will do. Several types of model glue are available for use with plastic, as are aquarium cement and clear silicone sealers for glass (pet stores and glass-supply dealers can offer recommendations here).

Making angle cuts can be one of the most exasperating problems for the hand-tool user. In order to make precise, identical cuts in two separate boards that are to be constructed parallel to one another, as in roof sections or glass grooves in opposing sides, each separate cut must be made in exactly the same way to insure perfect mating in the completed design. The answer to this perplexing problem? The jig.

Jigs are constructions, usually with some combination of clamps

---

[9]Forest Products Laboratory, *Wood Handbook: Wood as an Engineering Material*, U.S.D.A. Agriculture Handbook No. 72, rev. ed. (Washington, D.C.: U.S. Government Printing Office, 1974), p. 7-5.

[10]*Ibid.*

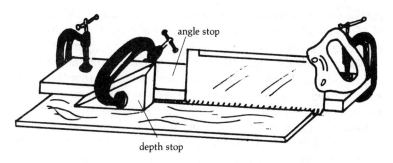

Fig. 6. Using a jig to saw a channel for glass inserts.

and wood blocks, that act as guides for the cutting edge of the saw or bit. Since the jig only guides and is not a part of the cutting operation, it remains unchanged. Each time it is clamped to a new work piece, it will guide the tool in making a cut identical with the previous one. Especially helpful in commercial operations where a hundred or a thousand cuts must be made the same way each day, jigs are also indispensable aids to the smallest shop.

The simplest form of jig is a guide block, cut usually from a two-by-four or other thick lumber to the angle desired (a friend with power tools or many lumber companies and cabinet shops can do this). After the guide block is temporarily clamped or bradded to the work piece, the cutting blade of a stiff, short saw (e.g., a backsaw) is carefully laid against this angle and slowly drawn across the work piece. Jigs may also be used to cut boards to a preset length, drill to an exact depth, or perform other operations (Fig. 6).

Most feeder designs call for two roof sections or sides of identical dimensions or for identical treatment of two parts, such as drilling a dowel hole at exactly the same point on two opposing sides. By bradding or clamping pieces together, both operations can be achieved at once. Extreme caution should be exercised, however, to be sure the edges of the individual pieces are carefully aligned. The technique works best on thinner woods, and power tools should not be hurried or forced through the cutting operation, as some blade deflection and consequent misalignment of the cuts may occur.

If a circular saw is used on plywood, special plywood-rated blades are available for smoother cuts. The good, or finished, side of the plywood is also usually placed face down when cutting, for a cleaner cut. In similar fashion, for boring operations with all woods, a scrap block of wood placed under the point of exit for the drill bit will minimize splintering, particularly when using a brace and bit.

Woods or wood composites like plywood with a pronounced grain pattern should be balanced during construction so that the grain runs parallel on adjoining pieces if they are to be treated with a semitransparent finish.

Remember, too, that the width of the saw kerf varies according to the type of cutting blade. While of little consequence in most operations, this can make a difference if a number of repetitive cuts are predrawn on the same panel of wood. Each succeeding cut will vary from the marked cut line according to the thickness of the cutting edge of the blade.

Sometimes it is easier to allow for some waste where complicated angles are concerned in order to nail a section in place, and make the final trim cut afterwards, using the already completed edges of the feeder as a saw guide. The amount of excess trim will vary with the requirements of each particular design but should be at least ¼ to ½ inch to give the saw sufficient clearance to obtain a bite, or hold. For those long, angular roof cuts a single long board or panel can be cut down its center at an angle (typically 45 degrees). When one section is turned over and the two pieces are mated, cut edge to cut edge, they will form a roof with matching, properly sloped sides. If power tools are used, a single board can be ripsawn its entire length with an angle cut on one edge. The board is then cut in two and the cut edges of both new boards mated to form a sloping roof. In this way a larger, easier-to-handle board can be used, labor can be saved over that required for two small cuts, and there is less chance of misalignment of the cuts since the saw is adjusted only once and the cut made in one continuous motion.

Flat or nearly flat roofs can pose a special problem. Rain droplets may run over the edge and actually flow back along the underside of the roof and drip into the seed-hopper area. To prevent this, cut a shallow groove into the underside of the roof approximately ¼ inch from the edge. (A small ridge of silicone caulk may also suffice.) Water encountering the groove will have its forward momentum broken and begin to drip at this point.

The grooves or channels for framing and holding glass can be chiseled or gouged with hand tools, sawn, or routed. When sawing it is easier to saw the channel the entire length of the side and then add a cleat during final construction as a glass stop to adjust the height of the glass above the feeder floor. Of course, the channels can also be sawn to an exact distance that is shorter than the total board length (Fig. 6).

In final assembly operations glass alignment can be especially critical because of its inflexibility, and great care should be exercised to insure that opposing attachment points are correctly in place. Take a little extra time to measure and remeasure before hammering the last nails in place. Leave an allowance of at least 1/16 to 1/8 inch in groove sizing. This provides a margin for error without affecting the design. Normally the weight of a partially filled seed hopper will properly support the glass but if it appears too loose or rattles in its channel a small brad can be pressed inconspicuously into the groove where needed. Hardboard, the material used in pegboards, is available in sheets, or panels, in both 1/8- and 1/4-inch thickness. Inexpensive, it can be cut to the same dimensions as the glass and used as a temporary insert for quick, safe alignment without repetitive measuring.

Unlike birdhouses, bird feeders place few limitations on finishing materials or techniques. They may be brightly colored and elaborate lawn ornaments or very basic and simple constructions as you desire. As an alternative to paint, you may consider using any of a number of clear sealers,[11] either alone or covered with a semi-transparent or solid-color wood stain. It should be remembered, however, that, in most cases, the primary function of a feeder is to attract birds for close observation. Loud colors and overly ornate designs might detract from this purpose. In fact, if supply catalogs are any gauge of consumer demand, it appears that most individuals prefer clean, simple lines and dull or natural finishes.

Metal, like wood, will require some special attention. Copper, brass, and aluminum are resistant to weathering but all galvanized steel and iron must be painted with at least one coat of a high-quality metal primer and two coats of paint. The surface to be painted should be free of oil, grease, rust, scale, and, if possible, all old paint (if all old paint cannot be removed it should be scraped or sanded down to sound surfaces which will taper gradually into unpainted areas).

---

[11]Clear film or water-repellent finishes are not recommended for plywood as they do not protect against damaging solar radiation and they require frequent and sometimes difficult reapplication.

Rust-inhibitive primers are highly recommended. For proper paint adhesion on galvanized steel a zinc-based primer is required. You should have no trouble locating a primer suitable for galvanized metal but in a pinch Thomas P. McElroy, Jr., in his excellent book[12] recommends washing the metal in ordinary vinegar. Allow it to dry without rinsing and paint. I have personally tried this method, and it seems to work quite well. Once again, finish coats should, in general, be muted colors. Black and shades of dark green appear to be most popular for posts and squirrel guards.

As always, perfection is a worthy but rarely if ever attainable goal. Birds are far more forgiving of our mistakes than we are. Children in particular can profit from a feeder project even if the design goes somewhat awry. In time you may even find yourself cherishing these projects, "mistakes" and all, far more than the perfectly turned-out designs of a less fertile imagination.

---

[12]Thomas P. McElroy, Jr., *The New Handbook of Attracting Birds*, 2d ed. (N.Y.: Alfred A. Knopf, 1969), p. 48.

II. Selecting the Right Feeder

Types of Feeders

Feeders are most often classified according to the method in which the food is presented. Among the different styles are *ground and near-ground feeders, post-style feeders (including feeding tables), hanging feeders,* and *tree-trunk feeders*. There are also several *novelty* styles with limited use but nonetheless possessing attractive or important features that are generally hybrids of one or more of the aforementioned styles.

Ground feeders will attract by far the greatest number of species because the ground is the most natural location for food in the wild and because there are a number of bird species that almost never venture far from ground level in their search for food. Quail and pheasant are obviously in this group. Mourning Doves will eat from elevated perches, but their large size and powerful wingbeats often make this option impractical. Juncos, towhees, and some sparrows such as White-crowned Sparrows and Field Sparrows are shy about using elevated perches, as are Snow Buntings and Horned Larks.

While it would be a simple matter to cast food in any open spot and wait for the birds to arrive, this is seldom the best answer. For one thing, if food is not properly protected and meted out in correct quantities it can spoil or be wasted. Mice and other vermin that feed at night may be attracted to large piles of unprotected grain, and snow cover can render food unavailable at just the time it may be needed most. Seed can be covered by rain-splattered mud or infected with disease-bearing droppings from ill birds lured in for an easy last meal.

Enclosed seed hoppers overcome many of these objections by doling out seed just as it is needed. *Near-ground feeders,* consisting of a flat surface supported by legs only a few inches high or split logs grooved to accommodate seed, require more frequent filling but can be easily swept clean of old hulls and debris or of fresh snow before refilling, reducing the chances of the spread of an avian disease.

Post-style feeders are stationary, elevated feeding stations. Five feet is the preferred height, although *feeding tables* or *shelves*—large, flat surfaces supported at each of the narrow ends by an upright leg or post—can be as little as three feet high. Even many large birds can use a post or table feeder if the landing platform is especially broad or open and the footing secure. A slightly elevated edge is recommended to keep seed from being scattered or blown off as birds land and take flight or winds gust. Many of the same birds that use ground feeders will be attracted to post feeders, including cardinals, Blue Jays, grackles, wrens, grosbeaks, and others. Two advantages of the post feeder are that, with special excluder mechanisms such as those mentioned in Chapter I, certain pests can be restricted and that, with its independent support, weight factors are a negligible consideration. Also, post and table feeders can be installed directly where desired without reference to available overhead support.

Hanging feeders are among the most popular of all styles. They attract fewer species of birds than the above types, however, because of their free-swinging movement, which is unsettling for some birds, if not impossible for them to master. Most hanging feeders tend to be lighter and more streamlined, resulting in smaller landing perches and sometimes none at all. Birds with the ability to cling while they feed, such as nuthatches, chickadees, and finches, are its prime clients. Typically, small trays are added to the bottom of the feeder and directly below the perches to catch spilled seed, allowing birds a second chance to retrieve their meal and lowering seed costs (some of the best hanging-feeder seeds are also the highest priced). Multiple perches are often used because many finches, in particular, descend upon the feeder in flocks and may occupy every available position, all the while squabbling among themselves and temporarily excluding still other birds. Hanging feeders, by the way, are also the most common means of offering suet, which is often suspended in nylon-net bags of the sort in which produce is sold in the supermarket.

Tree-trunk feeders are those placed in close contact with trees, preferably established trees several inches in diameter. Their purpose is to attract those species of birds that feed primarily in

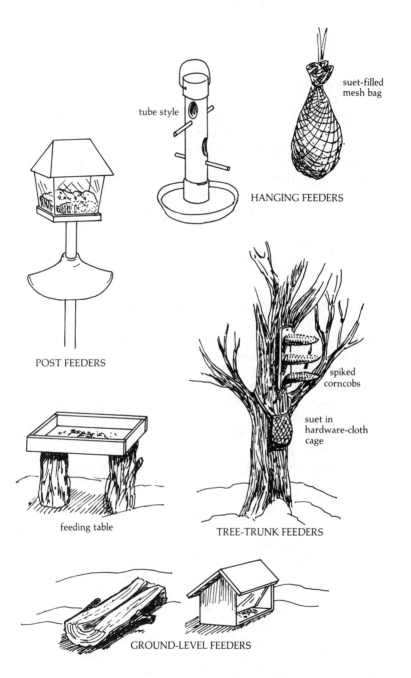

tube style

suet-filled
mesh bag

HANGING FEEDERS

POST FEEDERS

spiked
corncobs

suet in
hardware-cloth
cage

feeding table

TREE-TRUNK FEEDERS

GROUND-LEVEL FEEDERS

Fig. 7. Standard feeder types.

trees. Most naturally this includes the various species of wood-peckers and the Brown Creeper, but chickadees, nuthatches, and others may be attracted as well. Instead of seeds, suet (or beef fat) is the recommended food choice. Corncobs impaled on a nail driven through a board are sometimes also used to attract squirrels away from other feeders, and woodpeckers, Blue Jays, and other species will eat kernels or retrieve seed dropped on the ground.

It should be noted here that woodpeckers will also visit suet placed in other locations or attached to feeders or posts. It may take much longer for them to locate it, however. Moreover, suet will leave oily stains, particularly in warm weather, which may mar the appearance of some designs. Besides the common method of presenting suet in mesh bags, it may be melted and molded into forms or poured into holes in logs or decorative sections of wood.

Some of the most interesting and complex of all designs are the *novelty feeders.* They may present food in any of the four basic ways already described, but they include an added dimension based on some special feature of avian behavior or on a particular local condition that the designer wishes to exploit or correct. Among the most important variations of this style are (1) the trolley feeder, (2) the weathervane feeder, (3) the enclosed, or cavity, feeder, (4) the indoor feeder, (5) the windowsill feeder, and, finally, (6) the liquid feeder. With the exception of the liquid feeder, detailed separately in the final section of this chapter, each of these will be described at some length here.

1. Trolley feeders are built much as their name might suggest, with wheels or a pulley attached at the top to allow the feeder to be pulled either horizontally along a suspended wire or vertically from one height to another. In either case the idea is to change the location of the feeder gradually, day by day, without repelling shy bird species that might initially avoid either a second-story location or one too near a dwelling. Nevertheless, this design has proved less important than one might think. Given sufficient time and the right food stimulus at a stationary feeder, many birds can be induced to overcome their initial fear if startling sounds or movements are avoided in the vicinity.

2. The concept of the weathervane feeder seems to have originated in the desire to keep feeding birds sheltered in the lee of harsh winter winds and snow and ice storms. By the use of some type of bearing, a feeder can be made to rotate about a fixed point

through the action of the wind striking a broad baffle or baffles. In most recorded early designs the feeder rested near its center on a stationary wooden dowel or metal pipe. In between was a metal strip that reduced friction to a minimum when the feeder began to turn in the wind. There were two baffles, enlarged areas extending outward on either side of the single open side of the feeder. When the baffles caught the wind, the sealed, protected back of the feeder was automatically turned into the wind. More complicated designs may employ metal bearings (see Chapter IV for an example of this style).

3. Some birds that normally nest in holes will also use feeders of comparable design. These enclosed or cavity feeders employ one or more glass sides for viewing the interior at a distance. Among the cavity nesters that may use such feeders are wrens, House Finches, and chickadees. The food should be highly attractive (e.g., peanut butter, nut meats, or hulled sunflower), the entrance hole of sufficient size (from 1½ to 2 inches in diameter, with larger sizes attracting more species), and the interior floor relatively shallow and open to allow easy access and exit. Ideally the interior should be at least three or four inches square and no more than an equal amount in depth. While some species, e.g., chickadees, will pick up a seed and carry it elsewhere to crack, some will hull and eat at the feeder, requiring frequent cleanings if such foods are used. The wariness of many birds limits the usefulness of this feeder. Some birds, like the House Finch, may be noticeably uncomfortable in the brightly lit interiors of feeders with two glass sides. In test trials, this type of feeder was visited most frequently in winter, and even then only briefly and randomly throughout the daylight hours. Cavity feeders can be a lot of fun, but if observation is the primary goal a more open style is a far superior choice.

4. One of the most interesting of all the feeder styles is the indoor, or in-house, feeder. Originally called a terravium, it is based on an idea that originated more than a half a century ago. A glass box much like a modern-day aquarium is positioned inside a room with its open end attached to, and facing outward from, a raised lower window sash. Open to the outside and stocked with seed, this feeder will in time attract birds right into a room for close observation. As originally conceived, it was to be a sort of window on the outside world, with pebbles, a small bit of lichen or moss, a simulated pool, and perhaps even a clipping of early, spring-flowering buds. Currently they are used primarily as bird feeders, but they are a

wonderful idea for a person who is convalescing or for anyone who loves birds and has the patience and the opportunity to observe quietly.

A heavier glass, such as plate glass with polished edges, is generally employed. An old aquarium will do, and newer versions with acrylic sides such as those most recently marketed under the trade name Aviarium™ are not only shatter-resistant but much more lightweight. This reduces the strain on the window sash and eliminates the need for auxiliary bracing sometimes required with glass (usually a board or table-leg arrangement centered under the interior portion of the box and sometimes angled to slope back to the wall at some point—often the baseboard where attachment and removal are less obtrusive). This feeder design presupposes the availability of a double-hung window in a secluded portion of the house or apartment. Activity in the room must be kept to a minimum in daylight hours, as any sudden noise or vibration can send the birds into flight. Size is restricted only by the size of the opening available, but in general larger sizes made of glass should be avoided (commercial acrylic feeders may measure 24 inches wide by 12 inches high by 9 inches deep). The top should ideally offer an opening as a fill port, since access for refilling from the exterior of the house may be difficult. The floor is best made of wood, or an insert should be used to allow easy removal for periodic cleaning or refurbishing. If this insert extends beyond the outside of the window it can act as a landing and takeoff platform for avian visitors as well. Modern cements make framing a luxury more than an absolute necessity, but a wooden frame bordering the glass is highly attractive and can be painted or stained to match the decor of the room. Whether glass or plastic panes are used it is best that they have a reflective coating, but quiet viewing is also possible if all light sources other than the feeder itself are carefully screened and there is no back lighting from an open doorway.

As with all designs, the indoor feeder is not without some drawbacks. For security as well as safety an "L"-shaped bracket, angle iron, or corner brace should rest on the top edge of the raised lower window and be screwed into the sash or frame of the upper window. This prevents the further opening of the window either by a would-be intruder or by the inadvertent dislodging of the feeder. Ideally the top frame of the feeder should also be screwed into the lower sash of the bottom window to prevent unauthorized removal.

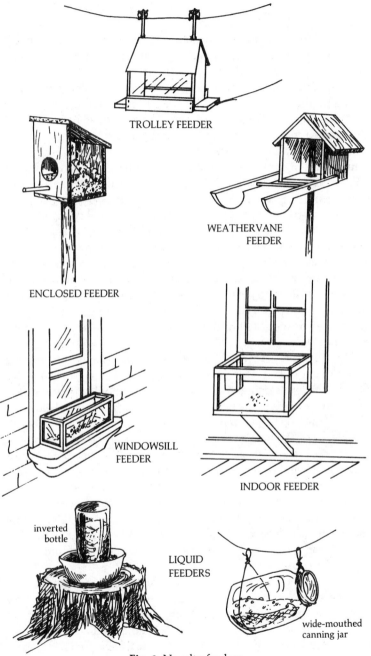

TROLLEY FEEDER

ENCLOSED FEEDER

WEATHERVANE
FEEDER

WINDOWSILL
FEEDER

INDOOR FEEDER

inverted
bottle

LIQUID
FEEDERS

wide-mouthed
canning jar

Fig. 8. Novelty feeders.

Since it is unlikely that the straight-edged sides of the feeder will perfectly match the window opening with its recessed track, some type of vinyl skirt (like those sold as replacement parts for window air-conditioning units) or acrylic, hardboard, or wooden panels may be required on either side of the feeder to seal the interior home environment from weather intrusion, but these adjustments will also make it more adaptable, allowing the feeder to be moved from window to window as inclination or necessity demands. In cold climates the indoor feeder will also likely have to be removed in winter, as moisture will readily condense on the cold surfaces of glass contacting warm, humid interior air. Room-heat loss is no small consideration either, in these days of high utility costs.

5. Windowsill feeders are a popular and less complicated alternative to the indoor feeder. Their purpose is simply to bring birds up close for easy viewing. They may be attached directly to a windowsill or ledge, or, if sufficiently small and lightweight, they can even be cemented directly to a pane of glass (some commercial feeders use suction cups, with mixed results). They may also be hung from wires or clamped or weighted to the window ledge for a less permanent mounting.

There are a few restrictions to this design. Usually the feeder is much longer than it is high (three to five times in many cases) with a flat or shallow sloping roof. The opening should naturally face outward, away from the house. Because the windowsill is below the normal standing height of most individuals, the feeder will be below eye level. For this reason the roof as well as the back should be of a transparent material, as it will afford the best opportunity for viewing. If possible the feeder should be easily accessible from the interior of the house to allow for refilling (some commercial designs ingeniously allow the entire feeder minus a quick-release mounting bracket to be taken inside for convenient cleaning and filling, but a top-opening refill port is equally effective). A broad landing perch is advisable as is a seed stop to keep gusting winter winds from raking the feeder clean.

One word of caution is in order. If the feeder is suspended by a wire be sure also to wire and secure the feeder from below. Few things can be more annoying than a loose feeder rhythmically rapping against a bedroom window late on a windy March night. Heavier feeder designs may actually pack sufficient punch to break a window pane.

6. Liquid feeders are the most specialized of all. Consisting of a plastic or glass vial or bottle capable of dispensing its liquid contents to the probing bill of a nectar-loving bird, this feeder may attract a few orioles, grosbeaks, warblers, or tanagers, but its preeminent value is that it is the only feeder that will attract hummingbirds (refer to the final section of this chapter).

Commercially Available Bird Food

As interest in bird feeding has increased over the years, so too have the supply sources of seed. Most garden-supply outlets emphasize feed and feeder sales in winter to even out their seasonal income. Discount department stores, supermarkets, and farm-supply dealers also carry seed. Local Audubon societies are an important and often economical supplier of seed, offering seed in bulk lots once or twice a year to raise money as well as provide a community service. Even some home-improvement centers may seasonally stock feed and feeders also.

Pound for pound, seed mixes are usually the least expensive seeds but frequently not the most economical in the long run. Many contain milo (sorghum), hulled oats, rape seed, flax, wheat, or buckwheat—all relatively unimportant and underused seeds which may be completely ignored and wasted in favor of the much more popular and generally more expensive millets, sunflower, thistle, and cracked corn. Specialty seeds such as safflower, which is attractive to only a few, yet highly desirable, species, may also be offered, but only separately rather than in a blend. Nor is domestic canary seed advisable, not only because it too is a blend, often including seeds undesirable to wild birds, but also because of its cost, which can be seventy percent more than that of the much more desirable white proso millet.[13] Be watchful also for inordinate amounts of dirt, stems, husks or hulls, and even gravel or small stones, which add weight without value. Old or deteriorated seed can sometimes be a problem, particularly with some "bargain" buys. Look for discoloration and for unusually light seed weight or loose

---

[13]Aelred D. Geis, *Relative Attractiveness of Different Foods at Wild Bird Feeders*, Special Scientific Report—Wildlife No. 233 (Washington, D.C.: U.S. Dept. of the Interior, Fish and Wildlife Service, 1980), p. 8.

seed hulls with evidence of insect damage (powdery residue and small, perfectly round "shot holes" may be evident), but remember that unhulled seed can stay usable for a year or longer under proper storage conditions, and a small amount of insect damage is normal. Most dealers are wisely honest and careful in their choice of suppliers, but even the best may on occasion get "taken" by an unscrupulous or unknowledgeable middleman. (See Chapter III for more information on the relative attractiveness of various seed types.)

An Audubon seed sale is one of the best ways for serious bird-watchers to acquire the quantity and variety of different seeds they require. If none is held in your area, a local club or organization may be interested in a seed sale as a fund raiser. Customarily wholesalers package seed in five-, ten-, twenty-five-, and fifty-pound bags, with orders required in thousand-pound or larger lots (a total that may amount to no more than twenty to twenty-five individual sales, depending on local demand). Custom blends may also be available. Check with your local or regional supplier for availability and terms.

Suet, an important food source, can be found at most locations that sell seed. It is sold in preprocessed cakes, balls, or other shapes and is often mixed with seeds or various additives. Unprocessed suet is available from the butcher or meat manager at your local supermarket. (While most meat-department employees know what suet is, some store clerks and cashiers do not. Avoid confusion and go directly to the meat counter with your request.) If you are a familiar, longtime customer there may be no charge; however, increasingly, stores are prepackaging suet at nominal prices in one-pound and larger sizes.

Nontypical and Do-It-Yourself Food Recommendations

Because of the large quantities of seed required at many feeding stations, as much as several pounds a week during periods of heavy usage, it is not possible for most individuals to grow their own seed. They can, however, supplement their purchases with homegrown seed of some of the more expensive varieties, particularly sunflower seed. It should be remembered, however, that such seed must be protected from premature harvest by both squirrels and birds. Remember, too, that processed seed has been graded for conformity to certain size standards. Depending on the variety you choose and on local growing conditions, you may find the seed to be unexpectedly large, perhaps necessitating adjustments in seed-hopper exit openings.

Peanut butter is too expensive for casual use but can be a real favorite with chickadees, juncos, Tree Sparrows, and others. By placing small portions in awkward places, a limited supply of food can be restricted to more desirable species. For example, this author has often watched Carolina Chickadees hang upside down to pick at peanut butter packed in the crevices of old pine cones.

Whole peanut kernels are eaten readily by Blue Jays, Tufted Titmice, and even White-throated Sparrows. In addition to conventional sources some very unconventional ones may be near at hand. For instance, candy and peanut-butter manufacturers and some large bakeries use literally railcar loads of peanuts every year. Because standards for human consumption are very strict, parts of some shipments may be rejected as a result of carton damage, rodent or insect contamination, or other defects that do not affect avian usage. Sometimes local policy or insurance regulations may allow for no recourse but the destruction of the damaged goods. In other cases, however, a middleman or salvage agent purchases damaged bulk cartons (which may weigh many hundreds of pounds) refused by the consignee and cleans or removes damaged portions for repackaging in smaller units for retail trade. Naturally the occurrence of such damage is unpredictable but may be worth investigating if such shipments are made in your area. A word of caution however. Be discreet. Despite its inevitability, no shipper, storage warehouse, or factory likes to admit that damage in any form ever occurs (witness the coy terms like "distressed merchandise," "floor model," and "demonstrator" sometimes used in retail-sale ads), and the salvage agents prefer not to be too widely known since such knowledge would drive down the price of their products at resale. Know what price you're willing to pay, plan to buy ten pounds or more and pick your order up in person, and hope for a friendly clerk at a storage warehouse, common carrier, or local cartage company who can direct you to the right person or see that they get your request.

Nut meats are pricey but can be especially attractive to cardinals, nuthatches, and titmice as well as Blue Jays, chickadees, and even wrens. They can be purchased for direct use or supplied from the refuse of your own holiday cooking preparations. Shells should be thoroughly cracked open so that the kernels are visible and accessible, but these do not have to be completely removed from the shells, as many species can effectively pick among the debris with their beaks, a natural nut pick. A number of native American nut trees also offer free sources of supply (be sure to seek the landowner's permission and leave some behind for wildlife and reseeding). All in all, nut gathering can be a great family adventure for those cool autumn days. Black walnuts are a widespread and popular favorite for both human and avian consumption but be aware that the green hulls can leave a dark stain on unprotected hands that will last for several weeks. Nut meats will spoil in time after shelling and should not be mixed with seeds or stored for long periods without refrigerating or freezing.

Berries—fresh, dried, or frozen—are favorites for many birds, including American Robins, Cedar Waxwings, and mockingbirds. Birds show little favoritism and will eat commercially grown cherries, blueberries, and raspberries just as readily as their wild counterparts. Among dried berries, dogwoods, viburnums, mountain ash, bittersweet, and bayberries are possibilities. Raisins are accepted by many fruit lovers and can be served whole or chopped into smaller portions. Pokeberries and viburnums among others reportedly freeze well but should be wrapped in individual portions so that the entire quantity does not have to be thawed at once. *(Be sure each package is clearly marked since some wild berries and in particular pokeberries are rated as poisonous for human consumption!)*

Orange halves skewered on a pointed wooden dowel attached to a feeder or board will attract Northern ("Baltimore" or "Bullock's") Orioles and Rose-breasted Grosbeaks, as well as Gray Catbirds, Blue Jays, and perhaps even flickers as well. Similarly, partially peeled bananas in open, clearly visible areas may attract tanagers in time. Bananas spoil rapidly, however, and should only be used sparingly. Apples, when cut into small portions, may be offered alone or mixed with chunks of citrus and other fruits. Even bits of date, fig, or prune may be used.

Bread, pastry crumbs, and stale popcorn are familiar offerings in suburban yards throughout North America. White bread is also a favorite with ducks and goldfish at parks and wildlife preserves.

Bread and pastry products are available at reduced prices at "thrift" stores selling so-called day-old bakery products in many midsize and larger metropolitan areas. Late in the sales day further price reductions or two-for-one deals may be offered to move merchandise otherwise destined for disposal. It should be noted that some bird lovers worry that white bread is not sufficiently nutritious for sustained usage. Yet birds, like people, do not restrict themselves to only one food in the wild, and its popularity prevents any one bird from totally monopolizing the food source in any case. Bread is simply a treat, and birds will move on to other food sources as the need arises.

Ear corn impaled on large (or spike) nails or wooden skewers on boards will attract squirrels away from other feeders. Woodpeckers, Blue Jays, and other birds will find attractive either the ears themselves or the errant loose kernels which may be dropped by other species. Field corn, Indian corn, popcorn, or sweet corn may be used and are available commercially, or you can grow your own. Local farmers may also supply ears at less than retail prices.

Suet, as already noted, is beef fat. It is the best and sometimes only food which primarily insect-feeding birds will take at your feeding station. Woodpeckers (including Northern Flickers), nuthatches, titmice, Brown Creepers, Northern Mockingbirds, chickadees, and even reportedly Golden-crowned Kinglets may sample it. It can be offered as is, straight from the supermarket, in lump form or chopped into small, bite-size bits, or it can be processed to remove less digestible portions and form a liquid that can be mixed with other foods or used alone and poured into molds to harden.

To process suet: (1) Chop or grind into small pieces. Use at least a pound if available. There will probably be a lot of stringy waste after heating, and larger portions will last longer—this isn't the kind of job you want to do every two weeks. (2) Heat in a double boiler. (For noncooks, a double boiler is simply a pot or saucepan that fits inside a larger one in which water is boiled.) (3) Pour off the liquid and discard any stringy residue that remains. (4) To increase hardness, cool the liquid until firm, and then reheat a final time. (5) The liquid fat can be poured into any reasonably stiff and waterproof mold desired, from the cut-off bottoms of wax cartons, to muffin tins, to used aluminum trays and pans, and even forms made from aluminum foil temporarily stiffened about its outside perimeter with cardboard or other device to maintain rigidity and avoid spills. (Note:

Hot fat is very invasive. It is best to let the liquid cool until nearly congealed. In that way it will harden more quickly. In winter it can be poured into forms placed outdoors on a cold surface to speed cooling and minimize the effects of spills or leaks.) Before hardening, suet can also be poured, or pressed when thickened, into holes drilled in logs or posts for ready-to-hang suet feeders.

Much has been made over the years about suet-cake recipes using seeds, raisins, corn- or oatmeal, cooked noodles or spaghetti, bits of fruit, milk, egg, nuts, sugar, and various other exotic and imaginative ingredients. It should be remembered, however, that the birds most attracted to, and most needful of, suet are for the most part not seed eaters. Their digestive systems and their innate behavior are simply not programmed for seeds. For instance, on several occasions this author has witnessed a mockingbird literally raking sunflower chips off a suet cake with its beak in order to get to the suet layered just below the surface. It is far better to mix high-protein additives like canned dog food, dehydrated eggs, or peanut butter into suet cakes than seeds or cereal grains. If you prefer, seed-bearing suet cakes can be mixed and made up at the same time as those for more traditional suet lovers, the birds whose summer diet is normally insects and berries.

Among less common food alternatives, bacon drippings make a high quality fat that can be congealed in cups or poured over seeds as with suet. Fat trimmings from the kitchen are less common now, as consumers demand leaner cuts of meat, but they too can be used (they are, after all, suet that has escaped the butcher's knife). Melon seeds are much less attractive than sunflower seeds but will receive attention. Finely broken dog biscuit or dry food can also be used, as can kitchen scraps (some authorities recommend trying everything from celery leaves and boiled potato to fried fish and cooked egg). Be careful not to put out too much at one time, however. It is unsightly and can attract vermin or stray pets.

Two nonfood items are also sometimes supplied at feeders in small quantities and kept separate from the food. These are grit (small gravel, crushed brick mortar, finely crushed oyster or clam shell, or coarse sand), which aids digestion and in some cases acts as a mineral supplement (farm-supply and pet stores sell grit for chickens or pet birds, or you can gather your own), and salt. Coarse salt, such as road salt, is reportedly especially liked by northern finches like the Pine Siskin.

The Hummingbird

Few other birds capture the imagination quite like the hummingbird, with its diminutive size, bright colors, and flashy, acrobatic flying feats. Perhaps, too, its relative scarcity adds to our wonder for of the more than three hundred species in the world (all in the Western Hemisphere) only sixteen are resident during the breeding season or year-round above Mexico and only one, the Ruby-throated, regularly visits eastern North America. Some, like the Buff-bellied and the Berylline, venture into only one or two southwestern states, with very occasional sightings in other areas.

The diet of hummingbirds is exceptional, too, consisting of floral nectar and various small insects found about flowers and on the bark or leaves of trees or caught on the wing from the air. Ruby-throats have also been seen about Yellow-bellied Sapsucker holes, where they undoubtedly capture insects and may sample the sugary sap as well.

Such a menu might seem daunting to the would-be hummer enthusiast, but in the early part of this century an amazing discovery was made that revolutionized the way in which hummingbirds were attracted and cared for in the wild. It was found that simple sugar water in small bottles would satisfy their thirst for sweets. We now know that the best formula for this mixture is one part cane sugar to four parts water. Odd as it may seem, don't use honey. It has been credited with causing everything from tongue swelling (due to fermentation of undissolved portions) and consequent starvation to liver tumors in hummingbirds. Many excellent commercial nectar mixes are on the market but don't be intimidated by dire warnings about the inadequate nutritional value of sugar alone. Unquestionably proper protein or other dietary supplements are to be desired, but wild birds do not feed exclusively at feeders. Sugar water is an energy-rich food quite similar chemically to the glucose-fructose-sucrose composition of nectar. Hummers will still hunt for protein in the form of insects and quite probably sample flowers as well.

Should nectar or sugar water be dyed red? This question is often asked. Because red has proven attractive to hummers in the past, many commercial nectar mixes are dyed red with food coloring to enhance their visibility. Since most feeders also have other bright markings this is hardly necessary. It might also be surprising to learn that feeding tests have shown that there is no evidence of an innate preference for red among hummingbirds. Red is effective partly because it contrasts well with green background vegetation and thus is considered the most conspicuous color in daylight. Hummingbirds might also single out red flowers first for close examination because red or red-and-yellow combinations are the predominant hummingbird-flower color of western America. Preconditioned by earlier contact with red flowers, hummingbirds arriving in a new area for the first time may seek similar-appearing objects in a strange environment. Further, tests of red, green, blue, yellow, and colorless solutions show that hummingbirds are not limited in their choice to one color and will sample the nectar capabilities of a wide range of flower types and colors.[14]

Just as the hummingbird is tolerant of color, so is it of feeder design. The standard formula for feeder construction is a tubular-shaped opening (matching the floral tube of many nectar-rich flowers) and colored red or orange. Yet many a successful feeder is no more than a wide-mouthed jar wrapped in a homemade wire harness and hung at approximately a 45-degree angle in an open area, preferably near flowers. Other designs use test tubes, pill bottles—virtually any container that will hold liquid and can be easily cleaned and filled. Commercially, feeders most typically use inverted bottles with shallow pans or narrow, bent tubes which employ the physical laws of atmospheric pressure and partial vacuums created by escaping fluid to prevent the contents from leaking out.

Simulated plastic or wooden flower petals painted brightly, while not mandatory, can enhance the attractiveness of any design as well as serve as a kind of flag announcing the feeder's presence at much greater distances. Restrictive openings can also limit the intrusion of bees or wasps, a problem that seems more prevalent late in the local growing season. Most North American hummingbirds have thin, rapier-like bills in the range of 17 to 21 mm long[15] (approximately $11\frac{1}{16}$ to $13\frac{1}{16}$ inch) and long tongues that can be extended varying distances into a flower to extract nectar. Anna's Hummingbird has a

[14]Richard S. Miller and Richard Elton Miller, "Feeding Activity and Color Preference of Ruby-throated Hummingbirds," *The Condor*, Vol. 73 (1971), No. 3, p. 310.

[15]Karen A. Grant and Verne Grant, *Hummingbirds and Their Flowers* (N.Y.: Columbia University Press, 1968), p. 26.

bill diameter of 1.5 mm[16] (about ¹⁄₁₆ inch). This means that bee guards can be added with multiple openings in the range of ⅛ to ¼ inch square where required and tube depths can approach one inch. (Commercial bee guards can also be purchased separately and adapted to individual designs.) These are only guides to limiting factors, however. Feeders should be as open, and nectar acquisition as easy as possible unless local conditions warrant change.

Sugar water is also highly perishable and will ferment quickly in warm weather. Avoid hanging the feeder in direct sunlight and change the contents at least weekly (independent trials by this author required fresh solution every three days in hot weather). Using boiling water may retard spoilage when premixing a new batch but be sure it has cooled before adding to feeders. Feeders must also be kept clean and as sterile as possible and should be rinsed as thoroughly after cleaning as your own drinking glass. Ants can be a particular problem. When refilling feeders, avoid spills that will alert them to search for the source. Coating hanger wires with salad oil or a tacky substance will often but, unfortunately, not always deter them. In severe cases the feeder may have to be relocated.

I sometimes envy my Western cousins who have so many more species to lure to their feeders. It can be quite a challenge to lure the Ruby-throated Hummingbird to Eastern gardens. East or West, however, a few tips will insure greater success. (1) Be aware of the arrival dates of hummingbirds in your area. Only the Anna's Hummingbird is widely resident over its range and it makes little sense to put out feeders prematurely or too late. Local Audubon Societies or other wildlife organizations and alert sales personnel at stores selling hummer products may be able to help you. Dated but serviceable data can also be found in Arthur Cleveland Bent's *Life Histories of North American Cuckoos, Goatsuckers, Hummingbirds and Their Allies,* available from Dover and at many libraries. (2) Don't let feeders run out. Hummingbirds are very location-sensitive. Once they discover food they will continue to look for it in the same area. Once it is gone they move quickly on. It is a good idea to keep a small bottle of solution refrigerated in reserve for those pressing moments when you simply don't have time to make more. Better yet, premeasure the sugar or a dry commercial mix in a sealable jar of

---

[16]*Ibid.*

known volume. When more solution is desired just add water and stir. (3) Increase your chances by using several small feeders to simulate the natural abundance of a blooming plant. Your sugar solution will also go further than in one or two large bottles or jars. After the feeders have been discovered they may be gradually reduced to two or three and only one will likely become the hummer's favorite. (4) Place the feeders near blooming plants, especially those known to attract hummers (see Chapter VI). (Although the evidence is not yet conclusive, some researchers feel feeders have a better chance of being visited if they mimic the color of nearby hummingbird flowers, wild or domesticated, that are currently in bloom. The theory is that the hummers are already finding food at a particular flower type, whatever color that might be, and tend to seek out this same color when investigating new sources of nectar.) After the feeders have been discovered they can gradually be moved to more advantageous viewing positions. (5) Be aware that the best chance of attracting any species is to present feeders in a location possessing the preferred habitat or natural environmental conditions for that species. Field guides can help here, as can your own personal observations on where a particular species is most often seen at a particular time of year.

Now that the feeders have been positioned and filled there is nothing to do but sit back and wait. If there is no bee guard and if the feeder is sufficiently close to a stable perch, you may find yourself confronted with one more surprise: several other bird species will partake of this sweet refreshment, including orioles, grosbeaks, warblers, and tanagers!

III. ATTRACTING THE RIGHT BIRD

Virtually any bird can be attracted to your feeding station given the right food and method of presentation. There have even been extreme cases cited in popular literature of both hawks and vultures appearing at feeding stations. The goals and the opportunities for most individuals are somewhat less ambitious.

In every region of America there are various locally resident species that can be found in the same area the year round. Other species are summer residents only. They arrive in the spring, nest, raise young, and depart in the fall. Still others may be winter residents who have dropped in from more severe northern climes. In some cases they may be of the same species as local summer residents. The local birds actually move south, creating a vacuum filled by their cousins arriving from up north, but outwardly the populations appear not to have changed at all. There are also transients, or migrants. As their name implies, they are just passing through on their yearly northward or return journeys. Occasionally stragglers, isolated birds that should have migrated but for one reason or another didn't, and accidentals, birds blown off course or otherwise disrupted from their normal course, may appear. There are even invasions, appearances of birds, like the Snowy Owl, that range farther afield than normal because of cyclical fluctuations in the population of their prey, or birds that are affected by severe weather conditions or an unusual wild crop failure, which may drive them into new areas.

These then, make up the available pool from which to select targets for attraction. Stragglers, accidentals, and invasive species are too unpredictable for planning, but personal experience and use of range maps and field guides can help you determine the summer, winter, and transient visitors most likely to use local feeders. Remember! This does not mean simply the number of species typically seen. If you have never fed wild birds before, you will, in most cases, eventually find yourself feeding as many as *fifty percent* more species than you used to see about your home on a typical day before. Depending on where you live this could mean chickadees, goldfinches, several varieties of woodpecker, and more. It will take time, however, and an intelligent feeding plan. You must provide what each species wants and present it in the proper way.

One frequent complaint is the mobbing of a feeding station by a single flock of an aggressive species. The easiest and usually best solution is simply to set up several feeders at once, utilizing different types of seed. Because all birds have preferences, they will tend to congregate at those feeders that best supply their desires. Unfortunately, removing a favored seed will not automatically remove a less desirable species. White proso millet is a House Sparrow delicacy, but they will sample other foods from time to time and feed more actively at other feeders after their primary food choice is exhausted. In fact, House Sparrows are quite remarkable in that there seems to be no commercially available seed that they will not eat, at least in small quantities.

House Sparrows, despite their squabbling demeanor, are gregarious and adaptable birds that can nest in reasonable proximity to one another if suitable nesting sites are available and may therefore be seen in some numbers about feeders at any time of year—although never as plentifully as just after the breeding season. Most other birds need much more room to raise their young and gather food, and their special habitat requirements may send them far from suburban feeders. As fall approaches, these birds begin to congregate in sizable flocks for feeding, protection, and perhaps socialization as well. In some areas of the country, mixed starling, grackle, cowbird, and Red-winged Blackbird flocks can number in the millions in winter. Rarely do they become a serious problem at suburban or inner-city feeders. When they do, they are quite susceptible to size restricters or other species-specific designs (see Chapter I), as are pigeons.

All species, from the stately cardinal to the diminutive chickadee, can be aggressive under the right circumstances. The American

Goldfinch is one of the most attractive of all North American species but once a flock descends on a lone thistle feeder they will squabble every bit as much as House Sparrows for the available perches. Like the proverbial barnyard rooster, songbirds also vie for dominance among their own kind. For sheer serenity few birds match the Carolina Chickadee, but on one unusual occasion this author witnessed a larger, dominant bird denying access to a safflower-filled feeder until it had finished despite ample seed and three additional perches. House Finches, too, can be quite aggressive.

What does it all mean? It means that if we are truly honest with ourselves we tend to dislike a species or prefer others over it less because it is "too aggressive" than because it possesses less remarkable coloration or it is too common, too successful, if you will, at living in the artificial environments we create about us. One bird lover may have eclectic tastes, welcoming each visitor as a unique and interesting individual; another may have much more narrowly defined objectives, desiring to lure only a few species. Neither goal is wrong, but the strategies employed are quite different. The first individual will offer a wide variety of foods to appeal to the greatest number of species, while the latter will want to deploy greater amounts of far fewer foods. Often the strategies are interlinked. Early on, feeding all birds will help establish which species are available locally. Later, more restrictive feeding will reduce populations to those species most desired.

To feed birds selectively, it is important to know something about their dietary requirements. Many birds are almost exclusively seed eaters for much of their adult lives. The American Goldfinch is one of these and it will not begin nesting until mid or late summer when wild seeds are more plentiful. Others, like the woodpeckers, are insectivorous, feeding almost exclusively on insects or insect substitutes like suet, although on occasion they may sample whole or cracked corn or sunflower seeds. Still others, like the starling, are omnivorous and will eat either insects or seeds without preference, depending on seasonal availability, while a very few, such as the Cedar Waxwing, are primarily fruit eaters. Fewer still are the nectar drinkers, the hummingbirds (which, however, also consume small insects).

Almost all birds require insects at some point in their lives, particularly during the nesting season, because insects offer the high nutritional value required for fast growth in young birds. For this reason, interest in feeders may slacken at this time as the rigors of feeding a hungry brood of nestlings keep the adult birds occupied. Soon the true seed eaters will be more in evidence, however, as the fledged young are led to the feeders as well. You may even marvel as a juvenile bird alights on the same perch as an adult to beg food that it could clearly have gotten for itself only inches away. Other birds, whose diet is primarily fruit and insects in summer, will switch to suet when winter deprives them of their preferred choice. Catbirds and mockingbirds are examples here.

Common Species and Their Food Preferences

Table 4 lists a number of common species and their food preferences. By selecting foods most attractive to the desired species or, conversely, least attractive to competing species, you may best plan your feeder design and food selection for the proper bird.

The table is far from inclusive. With more than six hundred species of birds breeding in North America above Mexico, only a very abbreviated list was possible. Yet birds tend to fall into very broad categories in which closely related birds will have similar diets—jays, finches, sparrows, for example. By observation or the use of a good bird guide or library reference the primary food preferences of any bird can be quickly ascertained. (You may even wish to initiate your own tests using a multicompartment feeder stocked with various types of seed.)

In compiling the table a number of sources were used, including this author's own independent food trials involving more than a dozen common eastern North American species. While the total results were broadly similar, there were occasional differences in the ranking of various foods according to popularity. In addition, not all trials used the same grouping of seed varieties or the same number of species, making direct comparisons impossible. The data must therefore be considered as a useful guide and not an absolute. (Birds may individually develop quite peculiar preferences on their own. One writer told of a bird that somehow had acquired a taste for ice cream!) Finally, no attempt was made to show all foods that a bird would sample or all available commercial seed varieties—only those taste preferences and seed types that are considered significant. As mentioned earlier, fillers like wheat, milo, rape, and similar seeds are of limited use.

What the Table Shows

There are a number of conclusions readily drawn from the table. One of the more interesting is the rather selective attraction to safflower seed. Cardinals, chickadees, House Finches, and White-throated Sparrows will dine on safflower when a majority of other species show little interest.

Niger, or thistle, seed, imported from India and Ethiopia, is also a selective seed and one of the very best for attracting the finches. Unfortunately it's also the most expensive and its per-unit cost may be three times that of whole sunflower.

Millet and cracked corn are among the most economical seeds to use but also tend to attract more of the less desirable birds.

Surprisingly, peanut kernels did quite well in attracting desirable species, while peanut hearts (milled peanuts broken into a finer consistency) did relatively poorly.

For sheer likability, oil (black) sunflower scored highest while both black-striped and hulled sunflower did well with a wide variety of species.

Perhaps the greatest revelation of this data is that several types of seed are required to attract the greatest number of species. If your budget is limited, this may mean purchasing one of the wild-bird food mixes. If so, be aware that such mixes typically have only five percent sunflower and often even less. Also be aware that a few birds, such as Blue Jays and Carolina Wrens, have a very annoying habit of raking through less desirable seed in search of sunflower. This can result in a good deal of spillage and more frequent refilling, but usually the spilled seed will be gleaned by other birds.

If your seed budget is more flexible, black, or oil, sunflower is one of the best seeds not only from a nutritional standpoint but also because the hull is tight about the kernel, leaving little or no wasted space and fewer empty hulls than in many larger-seeded varieties. Hulled sunflower is also attractive for hanging feeders but is much less restrictive than niger or safflower. White millet, yellow (golden) millet, and fine cracked corn are all nearly identical in the types of birds most attracted and are economical as well, but keep feeders filled with these seeds at least ten feet or more from those intended for other species. Otherwise, hungry birds denied a perch will spill over onto the safflower and thistle feeders—sometimes to sample seed but more often to perch and indirectly annoy other would-be diners while waiting their turn for perches to open at the primary food source.

TABLE 4*
Common Species and Their Commercial Food Preferences**

Family/Common Name	Niger	Black-striped Sunflower	Oil (Black) Sunflower	Hulled Sunflower	Peanut Kernels	Peanut Hearts	White Proso Millet	Red Proso Millet	German (Golden) Millet	Fine Cracked Corn	Safflower	Suet	Sugar Water or Nectar Mix
Pigeons & Doves													
Mourning Dove	S	S	P	S		S	P	P	P	S	S		
Hummingbirds													
(All species)													HP
Woodpeckers													
Northern Flicker												HP	
Downy W.				S								HP	
Hairy W.				S								HP	
Red-bellied W.				S								HP	
Jays & Crows													
Blue Jay		P			HP							S	
Chickadees & Titmice													
Black-capped C.		P	HP		S						S	S	
Carolina C.		P	HP		S						S	S	
Tufted T.		P	P	P	HP							S	

	Col 1	Col 2	Col 3	Col 4	Col 5	Col 6	Col 7	Col 8	Col 9	Col 10	Col 11	Col 12
Nuthatches												
White-breasted		P								P	P	
Red-breasted		P								P	P	
Wrens												
Carolina		S						S		S		
Mockingbirds & Thrashers												
Northern Mockingbird		S										
Creepers												
Brown		HP										
Starlings												
European Starling		P		S				S		S		
Weaver Finches												
House Sparrow				S	P	S	P			S	S	
Blackbirds & Orioles												
Red-winged B.				P	P		P			P	P	
Common Grackle				S	S			S	S	P		
Brown-headed Cowbird						P	P					
Northern (Baltimore) O.	S											
Grosbeaks & Finches												
Northern Cardinal							S	S	S	S	HP	
Rose-breasted G.			S							S	HP	
Evening G.										S	HP	
Purple F.										S	HP	S
House F.			S				S	S	S	HP	HP	P

Family/Common Name	Niger	Black-striped Sunflower	Oil (Black) Sunflower	Hulled Sunflower	Peanut Kernels	Peanut Hearts	White Proso Millet	Red Proso Millet	German (Golden) Millet	Fine Cracked Corn	Safflower	Suet	Sugar Water or Nectar Mix
Grosbeaks & Finches (cont'd)													
Common Redpoll	P			P			S		S				
Pine Siskin	P			P			S		S				
American Goldfinch	HP	P	HP	HP									
Red Crossbill		P	P										
*Towhees, Juncos, & Sparrows***													
Rufous-sided T.				S			P		P	S			
Dark-eyed J.	S			P			P		P	S			
Tree S.	S			S			P		P	S			
Field S.				S			P		P	S			
White-crowned S.	S			S			P		P	S	S		
White-throated S.		P	P	P	HP	S	P	P	P	S			
Song S.	S			S			P		P	S			

*Special thanks to Geo. W. Hill & Co., Inc., for their help in compiling this data.
**HP = highly preferred; P = preferred or well liked; S = satisfactory or acceptable; blank spaces may denote either nonuse or marginal use. Because the categories are somewhat subjective, not all authorities agree on the same relative rankings.
***Grosbeaks, finches, towhees, juncos, and sparrows all belong to the large family Fringillidae but for the reader's convenience have been subdivided. (Some ornithologists place the finches in a family of their own.)

IV. Detailed Design Suggestions

The following designs have been selected to demonstrate various types of feeders and methods of construction. A wide variety of materials were also employed to illustrate various possibilities. In most cases it is a relatively simple matter to adjust designs for the materials at hand.

It should also be noted here that with the exception of permanently installed glass inserts, such as that in the Hanging Cardinal Feeder, all glass sizes and glass channel depths are exact. In general, glass channel depths should be fractionally larger than exact measurements to allow for imperfections of the cut edges of the glass as well as for freedom of movement for easy insertion and removal. Not all craftsmen have the same level of skill or the precision equipment to make exactly measured cuts, however. Nor do all individuals agree on what constitutes a fit that is too tight or too loose. For these reasons it is always recommended that a test fit of the glass be made before final construction renders modification of the channel depths more difficult.

There is no one right way to design a feeder. The possibilities are limited only by your imagination. Don't be afraid to experiment. Birds are far more forgiving of "mistakes" than we are. Ultimately the true test of a feeder's value lies only in its use. If it is both accessible and acceptable to the birds for which it was intended, it has achieved its purpose and will provide many hours of unforgettable viewing enjoyment.

Portable Near-Ground Feeder

This simple design, consisting of a narrow shelf edged on each long side by shoe molding or a quarter-round seed stop, is intended for use when snow cover prevents access to other feeders. It can be spiked down into the snow and kept clean merely by sweeping with a broom, or, for a more permanent installation, it can be driven into soft earth before the ground freezes. If the snow is very deep, longer legs can be used (for extremely long legs or permanent installation, cross-bracing of the legs is advised) or the snow may be packed down before the feeder is inserted. Note that one leg extends much higher than the others to act as a landing perch and that the other three are level with the surface of the feeder to prevent wing interference when birds launch into flight or land. In independent trials this proved to be one of the most popular of all feeders, attracting many species that would not use an elevated feeder, so be sure to keep its above-ground height very small.

This is also an ideal father-son (or mother-daughter, etc.) project for those bleak Saturday afternoons of midwinter. A few tips will make this or any other project with young people more enjoyable for everyone. (1) Have all the necessary tools and materials ready before you begin. You will save both time and frustration—especially since very young children have short attention spans and often exaggerated expectations of the amount of work involved and the time required to complete it. (2) Be patient. You might want to underscore this one and repeat it silently to yourself throughout the project. It is one of the paradoxes of life that we are much less forgiving of mistakes made by those we love than by perfect strangers. Learning means mistakes. Don't expect perfection, speed, or immediate proficiency. (3) Don't rush in to correct every flaw. If the young person asks for help or will accept suggestions gracefully, fine, but don't take over because it's easier or the job isn't done *your* way. (4) Tailor the work to each child's level of skill. Every craft project requires some level of coordination, and coordination takes practice. Perhaps only a portion of the project will be suitable, and you and the child can divide the work into different responsibilities. For a very young child you may want to drill pilot holes and start nails, allowing the child to hammer them home. How about having him or her help you measure and draw lines, or saw with the aid of a miter box? (5) Don't forget the value of sincere praise. Never lie but

open ends for
water runoff
and cleaning

Fig. 9. Portable Near-Ground Feeder.

Construction Details

Materials   1″ × 6″ and 1″ × 2″ yellow pine;* ¾″ × ½″
hardwood "shoe" molding

	No. of Pieces	Dimensions
Elevated perch/leg**	1	16″ × 1½″ × ¾″
Standard legs**	3	12″ × 1½″ × ¾″
Seed stops	2	24″ × ¾″ × ½″
Feeder shelf	1	24″ × 5½″ × ¾″

*Actual dimensions ¾″ × 5½″ and ¾″ × 1½″, respectively.
**Saw points on lower, or bottom, end of all legs for easier
driving during installation.

if you look hard enough you can always find something to praise. Telling an eight-year-old that he did a fine job doesn't mean that you won't expect more of him when he is sixteen. His own ambition and growing awareness will lead him soon enough to discover that bent nail you find so difficult to ignore, and on his own he will purpose doing a more thorough job on his next project. (6) Display it. Give the feeder the same attention you would any other. Would you, as a painter, be fooled if everyone praised your ability but no one wanted to see your paintings? In time the feeder can be replaced, but for now it is a growth experience for your child. Don't minimize it by relegating the feeder to a dusty shelf in the attic or workshop.

Hanging Cardinal Feeder

This attractive feeder features a front-loading seed hopper and a broad, sturdy perch for larger birds. Note that the back pane of glass is permanently sealed into place by the long, overhanging roof, which directs rain away from the open front. (The leading edge of the roof is flush-mounted with the front edges of the feeder sides.) Ideally a small line of clear silicone or a paintable acrylic caulk will shield the edges of the wood next to the pane from all moisture intrusion. Remembering to install the back pane first, fasten the roof with either finishing nails (recessed with a nail set) or flat-head wood screws (countersunk for best results). Any exposed metal may be lightly coated with caulk and painted. For cleaning, the front pane is removable, allowing access to the interior of the box. Note also that the feeder is one-way. That is, because there is only one approach to the seed hopper, birds will never be blocked from the observer's view.

To refill, remove the ¼-inch dowel inserts (which keep birds from entering the top of the seed hopper), tip the feeder at a convenient backward angle with one hand, and pour seed in with the free hand. If safflower seed is to be used, a seed stop at the edge of the floor is advisable. (In test trials a starling developed the annoying habit of repetitively raking large amounts of safflower seed out with sideways motions of its head, as if never grasping that the feeder contained no food of interest to it.)

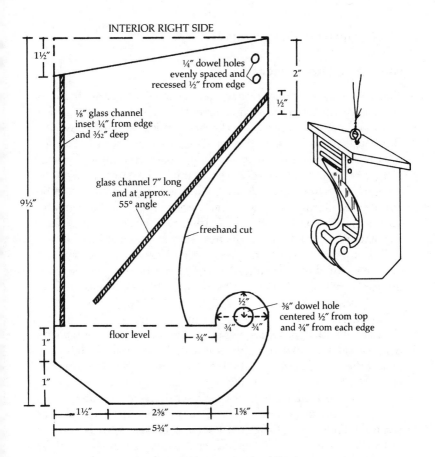

INTERIOR RIGHT SIDE

1½"

¼" dowel holes
evenly spaced and
recessed ½" from edge

2"

½"

⅛" glass channel
inset ¼" from edge
and ³⁄₃₂" deep

glass channel 7" long
and at approx.
55° angle

freehand cut

9½"

½"

⅜" dowel hole
centered ½" from top
and ¾" from each edge

¾" ¾"

floor level

¾"

1"

1"

1½"   2⅝"   1⅝"

5¾"

Fig. 10. Hanging Cardinal Feeder.

Construction Details

Materials ⅝" plywood; ⅛" window glass; ⅜" hardwood dowel; ¼" hardwood dowel

	No. of Pieces	Dimensions
Sides	2	9½" × 5¾" × ⅝"
Roof	1	7⅜" × 7" × ⅝"
Floor	1	3½" × 4¼" × ⅝"
Glass inserts	2	6" × 4⅜" × ⅛"
Perch	1	5½" × ⅜" dowel
Seed-hopper bars*	2	5½" × ¼" dowel

*Must be removable. Don't permanently attach.

Fourplex Cavity Feeder

This charming four-way feeder is a restrictive design with access limited to those species willing to enter an enclosed area. Such species include woodpeckers, chickadees, titmice, nuthatches, wrens, starlings, House Finches, Brown Creepers, and Weaver Finches (House Sparrows and European Tree Sparrows) among others. Naturally holes and interior spaces must be large enough to accommodate the species desired, and the food offered should be sufficiently alluring to induce entry. Levels of use may vary greatly both by season and by species. During field trials of this design, Carolina Wrens and House Finches were most often lured to the hulled sunflower seed (the finches were noticeably apprehensive and probably would have preferred a larger interior size), although an inquisitive starling did poke its head through the entrance hole on two occasions.

Note that the location of the glass panes requires a tight fit against the sides of both upper and lower floors to prevent seed from spilling over the sides. A small piece of compressible material, like felt, may be attached if the glass appears to be too loose, or the floors may be edged with a thin line of silicone or caulk. For demonstration purposes, the feeder body was made entirely from materials on hand, in this case, pallet lumber. The nonstandardized board sizes required some ripping (lengthwise sawing) of wider boards to arrive at the final dimensions. In such cases the sawn edges should all be turned to face outward on the same side of the feeder so that they will not contrast with unsawn edges. Notice the peculiar wedge shape of the seed hopper refill-port lid. A lid of this shape will have the tendency to remain in the down, or closed, position when not in use. To attach, drill a hole near the point of the wedge. The hole should be slightly larger than the shank of the attaching nail but not as large as its head. When the nail is driven home, a small gap should be left between the lid and the head. This will allow the lid to swing freely on the shank. Note, too, that there will be little or no extension of the roof below the top edge of the sides on the right-hand, or short-width, side of the roof, as shown in Fig. 11 (the left-hand side is wider only because it is extended by the thickness of the board used for the right-hand side). In aligning the roof you may find the following procedure easiest: nail the roof together as one unit first, then position it over one uncut side, and trace the roofline; this

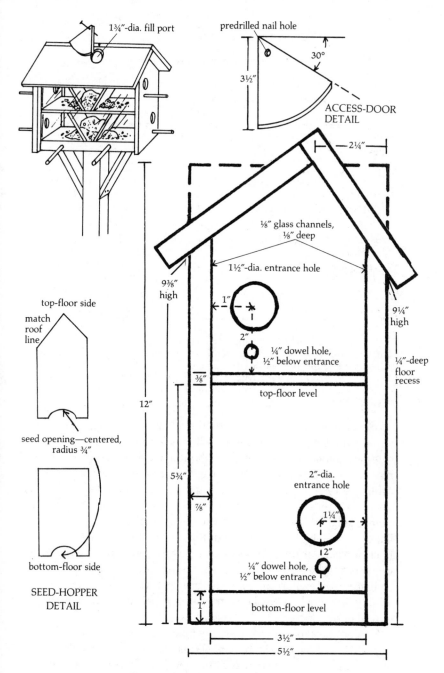

Fig. 11. Fourplex Cavity Feeder.

Construction Details

Materials   1" pallet lumber* × 3½", 4½", and 5½", respectively;** ¼" and ⅜"
plywood; ⅛" hardboard; ⅛" glass; ¼" hardwood dowel

	No. of Pieces	Dimensions
Roof	2	18" × 4½" × 1"
Sides	2	12" × 5½" × 1"
Top floor	1	12" × 3½" × ⅜" with 1"-dia. hole, centered
Bottom floor	1	11½" × 3½" × 1"
Seed-hopper sides—top	2	6½" × 3½" × ⅛"—trim to match roof line
Seed-hopper sides—bottom	2	5" × 3½" × ⅛"
Glass inserts	2	11¾" × 9½" × ⅛"
Seed-hopper access door	1	3½" × 3½" × ¼"—see Fig. 11
Perches	4	2½" × ¼" dowel
Glass stops (removable)	4	2" × ¼" dowel

*Actual thickness.
**1" × 4", 1" × 5", and 1" × 6" standard dimension board lumber can also be used if
allowance is made for the ¼-inch-shorter thickness. Chief differences will occur in the
height of the bottom floor and in slightly increased roof overhang over the entrance
holes. The refill port may also have to be lowered ¼ inch to allow for the thinner edge
of the roof at the point of attachment for the lid.

roofline can be easily duplicated on the other side. Then it is simple to
cut out the side pieces correctly. When the roof and entrance-hole
sides are joined, there should be about a 2¼-inch overhang of the
roof to act as a rain shield for the entrance holes. The seed-hopper
refill hole, or access port, centered on the lower roof piece, just below
the exposed edge of the other roof section, can also be bordered with
a small ridge of silicone to catch and divert water flowing under the
lid, or door. The hardboard seed hoppers are held in place by wire
nails or brads, or the floor pieces can be grooved to receive them, as
preferred. The top hopper sides must naturally be spaced to
converge somewhere outside the one-inch floor hole that allows
food to filter down to the bottom level, but spacing is otherwise not a
critical design factor.

Finally, the glass stops are simply long sections of dowel inserted
into shallow holes (¼-inch deep should suffice) for easy removal.
With the glass panes test-fitted into place, drill holes can be marked
at any convenient distance in from each side and just below the

desired final position of the glass; they should be the same diameter as the dowels or only marginally larger.

Post/Hanging Thistle Feeder

This versatile design can be attached to a post with screws or nails driven through the interior of the back when the glass insert is removed, or pegs can be attached to the sides for hanging. While thistle worked especially well in my test model, any seed type can be used if the seed opening is properly adjusted.

(1) To begin, cut a ½-inch downward slope into both the top and bottom of the two sides. (2) Saw the glass channels ⅛ inch deep and ⅛ inch behind the front edges on the inside. (3) Use one of these sides as a template, or saw guide, for the remaining, uncut side, which will become the back. Lay the side vertically against the long edge of the back just as it would stand in the completed feeder, and mark the angular cuts required to match the slope of the top and bottom edges of the back to that of the sides. Alternately, you can attach all three sides and lay the saw across the slanted edges to cut downward into the back. (Temporarily clamping or bradding a scrap board to the open side will provide more stability while sawing.) The roof back can also be trimmed in similar fashion for a flush-cut edge but this procedure is more cosmetic than functional for the roof and is therefore optional. (4) Test-fit the floor, mark cut lines to remove all excess projecting beyond the sides, except for the front extension, as seen in Fig. 12, and saw and attach. (5) Add hinges to the roof. Small, inconspicuous ones are best. In this example brass craft hinges like those used on jewelry boxes were used. Two were required by virtue of their small size. They were attached to the outside of the back and the underside of the roof, rendering the attachment points invisible from the front. (6) Drill a small hole in the roof about ½ inch from one of the front corners. On the same side as this roof hole install a dowel as a tie-down peg 2 inches or so below the top of the feeder and ¾ inch from the outside edge. Insert one end of a short length of cord through the roof hole, and tie a knot to keep it in place. Tie a loop in the remaining free end so that it will just slip over the tie-down peg. (7) Finally, insert a small brass escutcheon pin or wire brad into one of the glass channels ⅜ inch above the floor. It should extend far enough into the channel to halt the downward progress of the glass but not be visible from the front. Insert the glass and you're done.

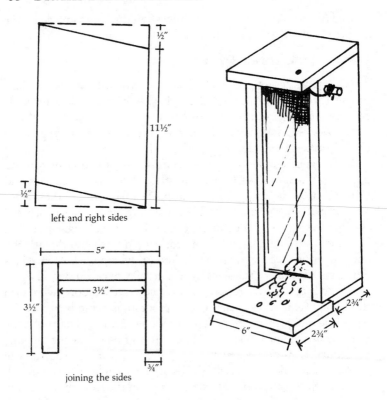

left and right sides

joining the sides

Fig. 12. Post/Hanging Thistle Feeder.

Construction Details

Materials   1″ × 4″ and 1″ × 6″ redwood;* ⅛″ glass; ¼″ hardwood dowel; small metal hinge(s); short length of small cord

	No. of Pieces	Dimensions
Sides	3	12″ × 3½″ × ¾″
Roof	1	5″ × 5½″ × ¾″
Floor	1	6″ × 5½″ × ¾″
Glass insert	1	11⅛″ × 3¾″ × ⅛″
Roof attachment	1 or 2	metal hinge
Tie-down peg	1	1″ × ¼″ dowel
Roof tie-down	1	small cord approximately 4″ long or sized as needed

*Actual dimensions ¾″ × 3½″ and ¾″ × 5½″, respectively.

Suet Medallion

The suet medallion is a circular ring of wood reinforced by a ¼-inch-mesh hardware-cloth center that holds the suet in place and provides additional perching area for the dining bird. If this feeder is suspended between two branches, the bounce or give that occurs when larger birds try to land, as well as the small perching area, will restrict the feeder's use to smaller or more agile species. If attached near or against a suitably forked limb, however, many more species will perch on the secure footing and reach out to peck at this tempting treat. If the feeder is carefully wrapped in aluminum foil, melted suet can also be poured directly into it, eliminating the need for a mold. When painted in brilliant shades of silver, blue, and gold, these feeders make lovely, festive ornaments that are eminently practical as well.

Naturally, the most crucial step in construction is the formation of the wood circle. There are three common techniques of manufacture—kerf-cutting, lamination, and steaming—but only the last will be considered here. Don't panic! That is the first rule. Although it may sound intimidating, wood steaming is not an especially difficult process, nor does it require specialized equipment. Despite the fact that many pieces of furniture about the modern home employ steam bending and shaping processes as part of their construction, this valuable ally is far too little understood by the average home craftsman. For this reason it will be described in some detail.

Wood bending through steaming begins with the selection of wood. Choose thin, straight-grained stock. Avoid pieces with knots, pith, or other surface defects, which might give under stress. Also avoid especially lightweight woods, which tend to be more brittle. A number of inexpensive woods can be ordered from craft houses in ⅛-inch thicknesses; however, similar material is available at little or no cost by taking apart shipping containers. Ash is a wood often used in crates, boxes, and withes; birch bends well, although its resistance to weathering is low. (The model for this feeder design was made of red gum found in the form of layer separations for pallets of brick in a brickyard.) Some of the best woods are white oak, red oak, elm, hickory, ash, beech, birch, maple, walnut, and sweetgum, although softwoods like Douglas fir and southern pine can be used.[17]

---

[17]Forest Products Laboratory, *Wood Handbook: Wood as an Engineering Material*, U.S.D.A. Agriculture Handbook No. 72, rev. ed. (Washington, D.C.: U.S. Government Printing Office, 1974), p. 13-4.

Once the wood is selected it should be cut into one-inch widths and into lengths suitable for both the intended size of the medallion and the container in which it will be steamed. (Finished size can be calculated simply with a flexible measuring tape or a piece of paper formed into a loop and then straightened for measurement.) The real advantage of wood steaming is that it can be done at either normal atmospheric or low-gauge pressure for many wood species. This means that the container doesn't have to be pressurized or have a tight seal. Almost any vessel in which water can be brought to a boil will do, from a large kettle, to a metal bucket or pail, to even a small trash can, as long as some type of loose-fitting lid is available to hold in the moist heat. Many liquid products, particularly caustic or inflammable ones like mineral spirits and lacquer thinner, come in five-gallon tins such as that depicted in Fig. 13. A simple opening with a lid can be fashioned by cutting three sides of a rectangle in one side (which becomes the top) with a sharp, heavy-bladed knife, such as a "hawk-billed" linoleum cutter, or with sheet-metal snips. The uncut side of the rectangle becomes a natural hinge. A heat-proof handle is then fashioned from a scrap block of wood and a wood screw, inserted from the interior side of the lid. A brick or any suitable weight will keep the lid down during heating. (The maximum length for a piece of wood to be inserted diagonally into such containers is approximately 15¾ inches, depending of course on the individual manufacturer's design and the condition of the tin. Test-fit for length before heating begins.)

The heating source can be an open fire, a camper's cook stove, or a gas-fired outdoor grill. *Exposed flames should be a safe distance from any combustible material and closely supervised at all times.* Indoor heating is not recommended unless a standard cooking utensil is available (it is properly sized for the burner and heavy enough to withstand the generally higher heat of concentrated flames); it also helps to have a tolerant and understanding spouse. Fill the container approximately one-third full with water. While it is perfectly acceptable to immerse the wood in boiling water, it is preferable to support it above the water level with some device (a coat-hanger wire bent into a crude rack is fine). Bring the water to a boil and prepare to wait at least 45 minutes to an hour before checking. Remove the wood with kitchen tongs like those used in canning, or with long-handled pliers, and test pliability. Depending on the wood and heat source, it may take an hour and a half or longer to reach maximum flexibility. Ideally several pieces of wood should be steamed at once so that they may be removed at different intervals for testing.

To bend the wood, grip it near one end with both hands parallel (you may wish to wear gloves). Using one hand to steady your grip, knead the wood by bending it downward with the other hand—but not too much. It only takes a small amount of bending throughout the whole length to actually form the completed circle. Each time the wood is bent, slip your grip hand a few inches farther along until the whole length has been covered. With experience you will soon have a feel for how far a particular type of wood will give without cracking.

Once the wood is in its approximate final shape it should be clamped to a rigid form to dry and set. Pipe sections work well and some, like the four-inch cast-iron waste pipe in Fig. 13, are free-standing. Or stakes driven into the ground in a circular pattern will do. The wood may also be clamped to itself alone, but some deformity will occur. Be sure that the ends of the circle overlap at least an inch. This will enable mechanical fastening later and will compensate for any rebound, or spring-back, that may occur after unclamping.

Allow several days for the wood to dry thoroughly and set into its new shape. Attach the overlapping ends by drilling a pilot hole and inserting a small eyebolt. Trim any excess overlap as needed. Waterproof glue will improve weatherability but should not be used exclusively. Apply several coats of a good exterior-rated paint. Trace the interior circumference of the circle on hardware cloth (a water-base marker works well and will wash off). Cut the hardware cloth *slightly larger* than the marked dimensions, being sure to allow for a cut-out area for the eyebolt shank and nut. Laying the feeder flat on a stable surface, press the hardware cloth to the center. The sharp edges of the wire should catch against the interior sides of the wood and hold fast. If the wire still appears too loose, however, colorful lengths of yarn or thread can be used to tie it in place. Insert a dowel close against the bottom inside surface by pushing it through one of the square openings in the wire mesh in screwlike fashion. At this point the dowel is only allowed to penetrate to the back edge of the feeder so that the feeder can still be laid flat for final preparations.

Now wrap the bottom and outer sides of the feeder in aluminum foil. Add melted suet. As the liquid begins to harden you may add small bits of sunflower chips to form a design or initial but not too much. Most suet lovers aren't interested in the seed anyway. After

Fig. 13. Suet Medallion.

Construction Details

Materials ⅛″ lumber; small eyebolt; ¼″-mesh hardware cloth; ¼″ hardwood dowel

	No. of Pieces	Dimensions
Circle	1*	12–14″ × 1″ × ⅛″
Center support	1	5″ × 5″ hardware cloth— approximate
Perch	1	3½″ × ¼″ dowel
Mechanical fastener/ anchor point	1	eyebolt—smaller sizes preferred

*Because of the effort involved and the possibility of error or accident it is recommended that several feeders be made at once. Any extras are easily stored or make handsome gifts for bird-loving friends.

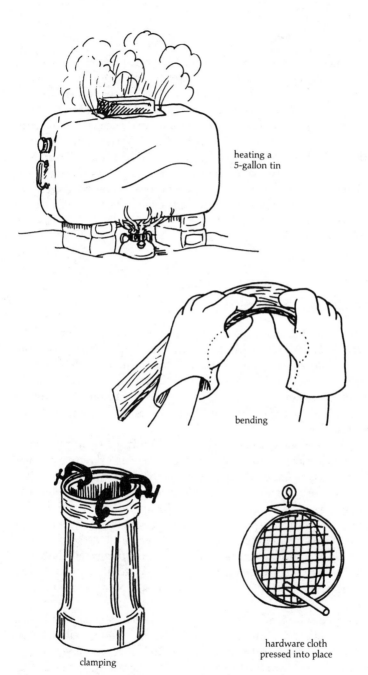

heating a
5-gallon tin

bending

clamping

hardware cloth
pressed into place

(Fig. 13 cont'd)

the suet is firm remove the foil and check for spills. They can easily be removed from the outside of the feeder by heating a dull-bladed butter or table knife under hot running tap water and lightly drawing the knife across the feeder's edge. Finally, screw the perch outward through the back until it extends an equal distance on both sides. Loop a length of thread or clear monofilament fishing line over both ends of the perch close to the edges of the feeder and tie underneath. Be sure to leave an extra-long piece hanging below for attachment to any convenient anchor point. (This will keep the feeder from spinning too freely. Or the eyebolt may be slipped over the tip of a branch and tied securely to prevent excessive revolutions.)

Hummingbird Feeder

No feeding station would be complete without a hummingbird feeder. This design features both simplicity and economy—important considerations when attracting hummingbirds for the first time. Chances for success are enhanced by multiple lures, and small-volume containers make most effective use of the feeder solution (one part cane sugar to four parts water—see "The Hummingbird," Chapter II).

Begin by making wooden flower petals from ⅛-inch stock. If hummers are known to be attracted to a particular flower blooming in your area you may wish to pattern the shape after them, but this is not mandatory. Nor do the "flowers" have to be especially detailed or authentic replicas. Hummingbirds will experiment, searching for that next new nectar source after their current one is depleted, and many successful hummingbird feeders bear little resemblance to their wild, natural counterparts. When painted bright red, the petals are in essence flags drawing the hummers' attention at a distance, and the feeder imitates the tubelike shape of most nectar-rich flowers.

The feeder base must be waterproof. Soft-plastic pill bottles are ideal for this and come in a variety of sizes. The "petals" can be wrapped around the sides or can be trimmed to a point and inserted in small slits cut into the top half near the neck or opening (see Fig. 14). If the latter method is used be sure the pointed ends do not

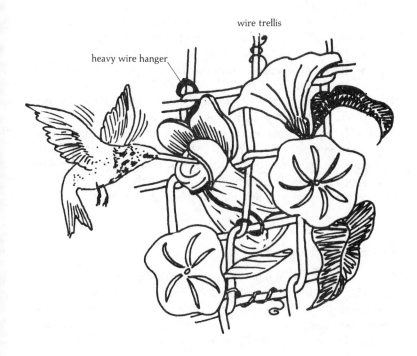

Fig. 14. Hummingbird Feeder.

Construction Details

Materials   ⅛″ lumber; small plastic pill bottle

	No. of Pieces	Dimensions
Flower petals	3	2½″ × 1″ × ⅛″
Feeder base	1	pill bottle (smaller sizes easier to keep full; soft plastic easier to work with than hard)

extend too far inside or they will act like wicks sucking up moisture within.

The completed feeder should be tilted at an angle of 45 degrees or less and strung from a wire or grouped on a pole near blooming flowers, especially those which hummers are known to visit. After hummingbirds have discovered the feeders, a smaller number of larger feeders may be substituted and the location *gradually* moved to a more convenient viewing site. Until then, be sure the solution is changed regularly to prevent spoilage, and avoid hanging the feeder in direct sunlight if possible. If bees become a problem, commercial bee guards are available or hardware-cloth restricters may be used (appropriately sized holes can also be punched in the original bottle cap). Ants may be dissuaded by salad oil or tacky substances placed on the hanger wires. In extreme cases relocate the feeder, and avoid spills, which alert marauding ants to the feeder's presence.

Weathervane Feeder

This entertaining design pivots freely at the slightest breeze to any point in a 360-degree arc. Once accustomed to it, some birds will even continue to perch as it moves, as if on their own private merry-go-round. The redwood construction is not only handsome and durable but lightweight as well, adding to the efficiency of movement.

Begin construction by cutting the wind baffle, a one-by-six-inch piece of wood pared down to leave a broad, paddle-like shape at one end. The pivot point is simply a plate-style furniture caster (those featuring brass plating and ball-bearing construction are the most efficient and weather resistant). Use a hacksaw blade to cut the axle and remove it and the wheel. The seed hopper is sloped slightly at the roofline to drain rainwater. Construction will be easier if the baffle is first centered directly under the middle of the floor (the outer or left-hand edges of both pieces, as positioned in Fig. 15, being flush). Fasten with finishing nails (the heads can be recessed with a nail set if desired and sealed with paintable caulk or putty).

Next, attach both sides to the roof. Invert the sides and roof, and, in similar fashion, invert the floor and baffle. Now nail or screw the floor to the sides (note that the lower edge of the pointed end on each side is flush with the left-hand edge of the floor as positioned in Fig.

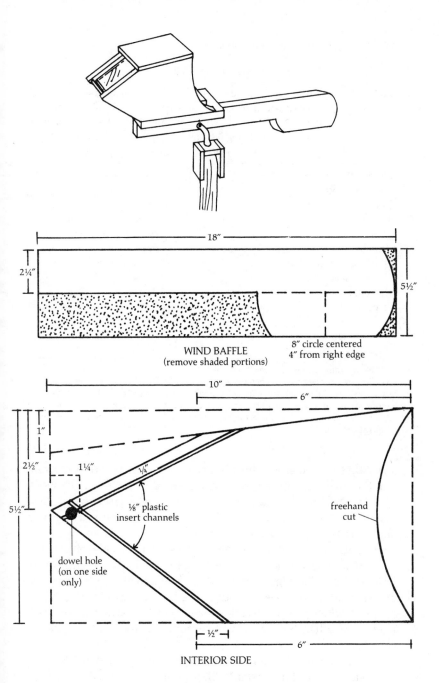

18″

2¼″

5½″

WIND BAFFLE
(remove shaded portions)

8″ circle centered
4″ from right edge

10″

6″

1″

2½″

1¼″

⅛″

5½″

⅛″ plastic
insert channels

freehand
cut

dowel hole
(on one side
only)

½″

6″

INTERIOR SIDE

Fig. 15. Weathervane Feeder.

Construction Details

Materials   1″ × 6″ redwood lumber;* ⅛″ plastic; ¼″ hardwood dowel; 1¼″
plate-style furniture caster (brass-plated with ball-bearing construction);** 1½″ bolt with nut and lock washer (bolt size
dependent on opening left by axle removal on caster)

	No. of Pieces	Dimensions
Wind baffle	1	18″ × 5½″ × ¾″
Roof and floor	2	6″ × 5½″ × ¾″
Sides	2	10″ × 5½″ × ¾″
Seed stop	1	4″ × ¾″ × ¾″ wood (excess from baffle piece may be used)
Plastic insert—bottom	1	4½″ × 4¼″ × ⅛″
Plastic insert—top	1	4⅛″ × 4¼″ × ⅛″
Dowel peg	1	1½″ × ¼″
Pivot point	1	furniture caster with wheel and axle removed
Pivot attachment	1	1½″ bolt with nut and lock washer

*Actual dimensions ¾″ × 5½″.

**Be sure the distance between the axle anchor points on the arms of the caster will
accommodate the ¾-inch thickness of the wind baffle when the wheel and axle are
removed, as there are several sizes and styles of manufacture. Finding a suitable
alternative should be no problem but do check before you purchase to avoid
frustration later.

15). Add the seed stop. This can be cut from waste left over from
making the baffle. Wire brads are suggested for fastening to avoid
splitting the narrow wood, or use pilot holes with larger nails. Now
install the two-piece plastic back. Note that the top plastic panel
should extend beyond the leading edge of the bottom section—
again, to prevent rain from entering the seed area. This top panel is
held in place by a removable dowel peg inserted into a ¼-inch-deep
hole on the inside edge of one side, as shown in Fig. 15. Because its
excess length protrudes well out of the hole, it is easily gripped for
removal when the top plastic panel must be extracted for seed
loading or when both panels are withdrawn for maintenance or
cleaning.

Finally, install the caster on any suitable base. Note that it is not a
good idea to insert the caster, without reinforcement, directly into
the endgrain of a post. A wooden frame between the caster and base,

something like that shown in Fig. 15, will distribute stress more evenly around the base. Now balance the feeder baffle between the upright arms of the caster, testing for even weight distribution (approximately four inches on center from the left or narrow-width end of the baffle). Mark and drill the bolt hole and install. Lubricate occasionally with a graphite-base product as required.

Five-Position Multiseed Feeder

This multipurpose design is ideal for those individuals with limited space, as one feeder can be loaded with any number of seeds without modification or excessive spillage. It is also economical, permitting the use of various combinations of commercial seed mixes. The roof slides off by means of a unique eyebolt-and-dowel arrangement, providing top-loading access that is both spacious and convenient.

The secret of success is the three interior awnings that cover the generous 2-inch-diameter holes. The bottom edge of each side should just touch an imaginary horizontal line tangent to the bottom edge of each hole. In this way the seed will flow down around the edges of the awning where birds may reach in and pluck it out, but it will not flow out of the feeder. Begin construction with ⅛-inch hardboard, which is both lightweight and paintable (flat black works well, or the wood may be left natural). Dry-fit the pieces in place, one hood at a time.

Now proceed with each awning as follows. Drill a small starter hole (¹⁄₁₆ inch) near the top center of the awning-roof piece and approximately ¼ inch from its edge. The hole should angle downward at about 30 degrees through the awning roof and into the feeder side above the access hole, but *do not* drill completely through to the outside. Insert a small brass screw (such as a #6 × ¾-inch) and tighten the screw until the roof is held fast (but *don't* finish tightening). Remove the awning sides. (You may wish to drill mounting holes for two ⅛-inch dowels at this time. The perch will extend completely through to the inside of the feeder to act as the middle bar. The ⅛-inch bars are evenly positioned, on the *inside*, on either side of this ¼-inch rod. All three dowels should be widely spaced and do not have to extend to the lower edge of the awning. Their purpose is simply to provide a sufficient barrier to keep birds from entering the seed hopper but not from gaining access to the seed.) Now place glue on contact points with the awning roof and feeder sides. Re-install. Continue to tighten the awning screw until it supplies sufficient pressure to clamp the sides in place until dry. Leave the screw in place as a secondary means of support.

Construct the sides (see Fig. 16) and glue them to the floor. Then cut and fit the glass inserts. To construct the sliding roof, begin by positioning and installing four *screweyes*, two on each wooden side. Each should be ¾ inch down from the top and ¾ inch in from the

Construction Details

Materials   ½″ × 5¼″ pine;* ⅛″ glass; ⅛″ and ¼″ hardwood dowels; ⅛″ hardboard; #6 × ¾″ brass screws; 2½″ × ½″ eyelet-diameter eyebolts; 1½″ × ⅜″ eyelet-diameter screweyes

	No. of Pieces	Dimensions
Feeder:		
Sides	2	12″ × 5¼″ × ½″
Roof	1	12½″ × 5¼″ × ½″
Floor	1	10½″ × 5¼″ × ½″
Glass inserts	2	11⅞″ × 6″ × ⅛″
Perches**	3	5″ × ¼″ dowel
Seed Hopper Awnings:		
Sides	6	2½″ × 2½″ (right triangle) × ⅛″ hardboard
Roof	3	3½″ × 2¼″ × ⅛″ hardboard
Entrance bars***	6	2″ × ⅛″ dowel
Attaching screws	3	#6 × ¾″ brass screw
Sliding-Roof Attachments:		
Slide rods (or dowels)	2	4⅝″ × ¼″ dowel
Dowel holders—sides	4	1½″ × ⅜″ eyelet screweye
Dowel holders—roof	2	2½″ × ½″ eyelet eyebolt
Hanger-wire eyebolt	1	2½″ × ½″ eyelet eyebolt

*This lumber was found in the form of old shelving. One-by-six lumber can be substituted with no major changes in the design other than recessing the glass inserts and screweyes an additional ⅛″ from the edges of each side.

**The perches are extra long so that one end of each can be inserted completely through the feeder side to the interior of the feeder—thus becoming the central awning bar.

***Evenly space one entrance bar (or dowel), on the inside, on either side of the central awning bar (the extended perch). The mounting holes should not penetrate to the exterior of the sides. Nor do the dowels have to extend inward all the way across the bottom of the awning opening. Their purpose is simply to keep some birds, e.g., House Sparrows and House Finches, from being tempted into entering the hopper as the seed level drops.

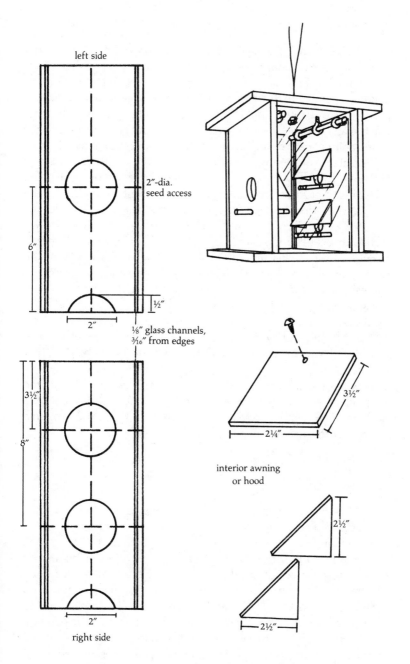

left side

2"-dia.
seed access

6"

½"

2"

⅛" glass channels,
³⁄₁₆" from edges

3½"

8"

2"

right side

3½"

2¼"

interior awning
or hood

2½"

2½"

Fig. 16. Five-Position Multiseed Feeder.

outside. Turn the screweyes down equally until they are solid and firm, but be careful not to overtighten, or you may pierce the outside of the feeder. Each pair of screweyes should be vertical, with the openings parallel to the glass sides. Test-fit dowels in both screweye pairs. Their length should just touch the glass sides or be only fractionally shorter than this. Now test-fit the roof, and mark the centerpoint of each dowel on the roof edge above it. Remove the roof and carefully draw horizontal lines across the width of the board between the dowel marks on opposite edges. Now mark the midpoint of each of these lines. Drill and install *eyebolts* (notice the distinction—screweyes might loosen and pull out when installed for use in a vertical position and subjected to repeated stress). Also install the central-mounting eyebolt—to which you will attach hanger wire—at this time. With a glass insert removed from the feeder, insert a dowel through the pair of screweyes and the corresponding roof eyebolt on each side. Notice that, by tightening the screweyes or eyebolts, various adjustments can be made in the tightness of the fit. For instance, if two opposing screweyes are tightened alone, they will pull one end of each dowel inward, effectively reducing the length of free travel of the eyebolts on that end of each dowel. Thus, the roof will slide open in only one direction—away from the tightened screweyes. (If desired, the protruding ends of the eyebolts can be cut near the nut with a hacksaw or bolt cutter to reduce their profile or they can be covered entirely with caps or ornamental trim.)

Acrylic Pyramid

This lightweight feeder features a see-through hopper with four-way access. The base is removable for cleaning and the weather-tight opening at the top is proportioned to hold a funnel for easy, spill-free loading. It can also be used as either a free-hanging or a post-mounted model. In field trials it was especially attractive when filled with white safflower seed, which contrasted well with wood parts painted black, and both cardinals and House Finches found it to their liking. Notice, too, the breadth and openness of the perches, which offer convenient landing for larger birds, high visibility to guard against danger, and quick-launching points for hurried flight.

Begin construction by sawing out the acrylic hopper sides. Be

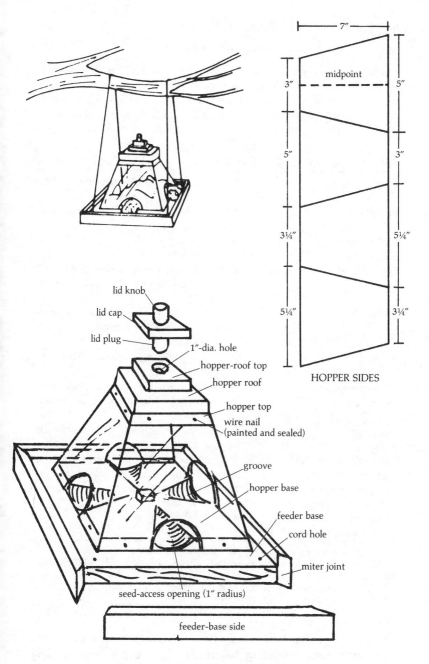

7"

3"   5"

midpoint

5"   3"

3¼"   5¼"

5¼"   3¼"

HOPPER SIDES

lid knob

lid cap

lid plug

1"-dia. hole

hopper-roof top

hopper roof

hopper top

wire nail
(painted and sealed)

groove

hopper base

feeder base

cord hole

miter joint

seed-access opening (1" radius)

feeder-base side

Fig. 17. Acrylic Pyramid.

Construction Details

Materials   ⅛" acrylic (plastic); 1" × 2", 1" × 4", and 1" × 8" pine lumber;*
1½"-long bolt with nut and washer (bolt size optional); small
brass wood screws (the smaller the better, but at least ⅜" long);
¾"-long wire nails; heavy cord for final mounting; acrylic-plastic
glue or cement

	No. of Pieces	Dimensions
Hopper sides	2	7" high × (5¼" base and 3¼" top width) × ⅛" acrylic
Hopper sides	2	7" high × (5" base and 3" top width) × ⅛" acrylic
Hopper base	1	5" × 5" × ¾"***
Feeder base	1	7¼" × 7¼" × ¾"
Feeder base sides (perches)	4	7¼" (inside length—bevel-cut at 45° angle from 8¾" outside length) × 1½" × ¾"
Hopper top	1	3" × 3" × ¾"—with 1"-dia. hole, centered (save cutout for use as knob)***
Hopper roof	1	3½" × 3½" × ¾"—with 1"-dia. hole, centered
Hopper-roof top	1	1¾" × 1¾" × ¾"—with 1"-dia. hole, centered (save cutout for use as lid plug)
Lid plug	1	1"-dia. circle—see "Hopper-roof top"
Lid cap	1	2½" × 2½" × ¾"
Lid knob (or handle)	1	1"-dia. circle—see "Hopper top"
Hopper-base screws	8	⅜"-long (minimum) brass screw
Hopper-feeder-base mounting bolt	1	1½"-long (approx.) bolt with nut and washer
Hopper-top fasteners	8	¾"-long wire nail
Heavy mounting cord	2	36" length

*Actual dimensions ¾" × 1½", 3½", and 7¼", respectively.
**Trim hopper base to slope inward to conform to the slope of the hopper sides.
See text.
***Trim hopper top to slope outward at the base to conform to the slope of the
hopper sides.

patient. If you want that truly finished, professional look, spend
some time carefully sanding the cut edges smooth before proceeding
further. Cut the seed-access or -exit openings (1-inch radius). Now
glue or cement the long edges of the sides together. Naturally, each

pair of sides with the same dimensions should be opposite—*not adjoining*—and the longer-width sides should overlap the edges of the smaller, 5-by-3-inch sides. (Be sure to remove excess glue or cement before it hardens.) The edges of the hopper base should slope inward and those of the hopper top should slope outward from their listed dimensions at approximately a seven-degree angle to conform to the sloping sides of the hopper. This slope is best created with an adjustable saw when each piece is first cut but may also be done afterward by trimming with a rasp, pocket knife, or wood chisel. (The top, of course, must be cut oversized and trimmed back to 3 inches at its top edge. The base should be trimmed down from its listed dimensions.) Next, test-fit the hopper to its base and mark the outline of the seed opening on the edge of each of its sides. Remove the hopper and incise a grooved or sloping channel within the boundaries of the premarked outlines. (This will help direct the flow of seed to the exits. The depth of the grooving is optional.) Drill the center hole in the hopper base and insert and loosely tighten the bolt and nut. Two pilot holes should be drilled at the lower end of each hopper side for attachment with small brass screws. Attach hopper to base.

The roof consists of two three-piece units, the roof proper and a lid. Construct the main roof area first. Begin by attaching the hopper top (which we will now consider to be the bottom piece of the main roof area) to the bottom of the hopper roof. (If you have already cut out the 1-inch central holes, be sure that one is centered directly over the other.) Now attach the third piece—the roof top—with its hole also centered. Be sure the center cutout is used to form the lid plug. Because it was cut from the roof top it will match and fill the hole without the need for trimming often caused by imperfections in the original cut. The nature of these same imperfections means that the next piece, the lid cap, should be marked for attachment with its plug temporarily fitted into the roof top, from which it has been cut. (If not, the lid cap may be out of square with, or positioned at an angle to, the roof top.) Since some rainwater may drain back under the lid cap, a ridge of clear silicone or a shallow groove cut across the exposed area of the underside will help redirect the flow downward. To complete the roof use the center cutout from either the hopper top or hopper roof to form a knob, or handle. All roof sections should now be painted with several coats of a high-quality exterior paint, as the hopper top will be inaccessible after mounting.

Attach the hopper to the bottom roof section (the hopper top) by inserting wire nails into predrilled holes. (The heads should be painted to match the color of the hopper top and coated with clear silicone sealer to avoid rust.) After painting, attach the hopper to its base with screws. *Do not* seal the edges with silicone, as the base must remain removable for periodic cleaning.

Now attach the feeder base sides to the feeder base. Miter joints look especially sharp and blend with the angular lines of the feeder, but butt joints are satisfactory. Allow the edges of the base sides, or perches, to extend ½ inch below the bottom of the feeder base. (This will hide the bolt hardware and the attachment points for the cords.) Drill a hole of suitable dimension near each corner of the feeder base for the mounting cords and also a bolt hole at its center. Bolt the hopper to the feeder base and insert the ends of two lengths of cord through the corner holes for final installation of the feeder. Knot the ends to prevent slippage. Although the seed is held safely above the feeder base by the floor of the hopper, some water may accumulate on the feeder base itself during heavy rain. For this reason a few evenly spaced weep holes between the feeder-base sides and the seed hopper may be useful.

Traditional Chalet-style Feeder

This durable, large-capacity feeder follows the classic lines of a typical chalet-style feeder. A novel seed-refill door slides conveniently out of the way for hands-free refilling. On either end, suet feeders in contrasting styles are additional, optional features.

Note that the roof pieces are bevel-cut at a 45-degree angle at the ridge line. Also note that the roof is *not* attached directly to the sides. Instead, a one-by-two is centered along the top edge of one roof piece. This cleat can provide extra nailing surface when joining the roof sections but it also serves a second and more important role. When a pilot hole is drilled through each side near its apex and into the cleat beyond, a screw can be inserted through the exterior of the side and into the cleat, thereby locking the roof into place. Whenever the glass inserts must be cleaned or the feeder repaired, simply remove the screws, and the whole roof comes off intact.

The seed-refill opening is a triangular section centered at the lower edge of one roof piece (the roof section that contacts the ¾-inch-thick edge of the roof cleat—not its 1½-inch width). A larger

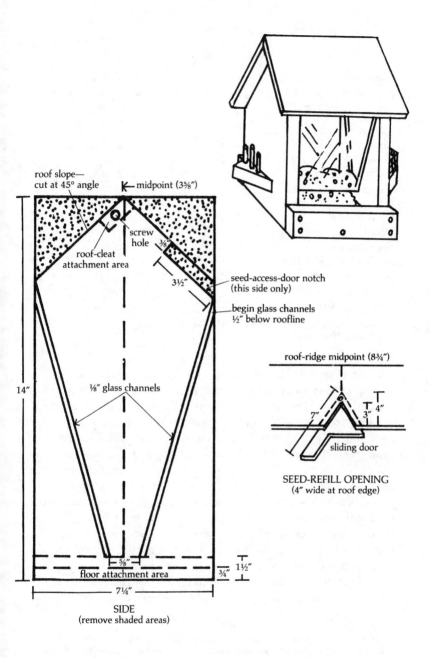

roof slope—
cut at 45° angle

midpoint (3⅝")

screw hole

roof-cleat attachment area

⅜"

3½"

seed-access-door notch (this side only)

begin glass channels ½" below roofline

⅛" glass channels

14"

roof-ridge midpoint (8¾")

7"

3"

4"

sliding door

SEED-REFILL OPENING
(4" wide at roof edge)

⅝"

floor attachment area

¾"

1½"

7¼"

SIDE
(remove shaded areas)

Fig. 18. Traditional Chalet-style Feeder.

Construction Details

Materials   ⅛" glass; 1" × 2" and 1" × 8" cedar;* ¼" hardwood dowel; ¼"
plywood; 1¼"-length (minimum) wood screws; hardware cloth
(optional)

	No. of Pieces	Dimensions
Roof	2	17½" × 7¼" × ¾"
Roof cleat	1	8" × 1½" × ¾"
Roof-cleat screws	2	1¼"-long (minimum) woodscrew
Sides	2	14" × 7¼" × ¾"
Glass inserts	2	8¼" × 8⅝" × ⅛"
Floor	1	8" × 7¼" × ¾"
Seed stop/perch	2	9½" × 1½ × ¾"
Seed-hopper refill door	1	7" × 4" × ¼" plywood**
Suet-feeder floor	2	3" × 3" (right triangle) × ¾"
Suet stop—one side	3	2" × ¼" dowel
Suet stop—second side	1	6½" × 2" hardware cloth

*Actual dimensions ¾" × 1½" and ¾" × 7¼", respectively.
**Trim as illustrated. See Fig. 18.

triangle with one side extended as a handle[18] is attached to the
underside of the roof as an access door. (Drill a hole, slightly larger than
the diameter of the attaching nail, near the peak of the access door,
working from the *inside* of the roof. Drive the nail home but leave a
small gap between the nail and plywood. A sturdy nail with a large
head should be used. If the shank is too long to avoid penetrating to
the outside of the roof—and it probably will be—cut the shank with
heavy wire cutters, a bolt cutter, or a hacksaw to shorten it before
installing.) The door will pivot on the nail shaft to open or close the
seed-refill opening while being supported by the nail head. (Note
that a slot must be cut in one side only, at the roof line, to allow the
free travel of the access door past its edge, thus permitting the
widest possible opening.)

The suet feeders are installed 3¼ inches above the bottom outside
edge of each end, using nails or screws as desired. Evenly space the

---

[18]Occasionally birds, especially flocking species, may perch on this handle. The
motion of repeated takeoffs and landings can cause the door to shift partially open. If
this should become a problem, see the "Post/Hanging Thistle Feeder" in this chapter
for one solution, the tie-down peg.

dowels on one in order to pin suet (or fruit in mild weather) in place. The other suet feeder is bordered by hardware cloth tacked to both its outer edge and the chalet-feeder end as required for stability. The top is left open and suet is inserted in sufficient quantity to allow access through openings in the wire mesh. Remember! Sharp edges of the cut wire should be bent down to prevent injury. Peanut kernels or other foods could also be used and accessed through the open top. (Caution: As noted in the text, suet will stain wood with its oily fat, particularly in warm weather.)

Chickadee Feeder

This feeder is named after the Carolina Chickadee, the only species—despite the lure of popular black (oil) sunflower—that consistently visited on a daily basis. With the exception of one House Sparrow, which made fitful and only partly successful efforts to cling momentarily to one side of the feeder and crane its neck upward to the level of the seed opening, no other species managed to solve the riddle of this species-restrictive design and even the lone House Sparrow made only sporadic attempts to dine, even while numbers of its kind fed daily at other feeders located only inches away. (Although I have tested this feeder in a region populated only by the Carolina Chickadee, probably it would also attract this bird's more northerly counterpart, the Black-capped Chickadee.)

The secret to the Chickadee Feeder's success is (1) the absence of a true landing perch, which limits access to species that can cling to the edge of the floor or feeder side while feeding and (2) a porch roof and extended sides, which restrict wing movements of larger birds and block visual sighting of the landing area. Many birds survey landings from above and do not sweep up and in as a chickadee can but rather drop down from a higher position to land. Bypassing the visual obstruction is for some birds the equivalent of flying blind.

Note the simple yet effective lock-down feature of the seed-hopper roof. A nail on either side is inserted through slightly oversized holes and into corresponding openings in cleats fastened to the underside of the roof. (The nails should be allowed to extend outward about an inch on either side for easy extraction.) Note, too, that the porch roof and sides are a single unit held in place by screws.

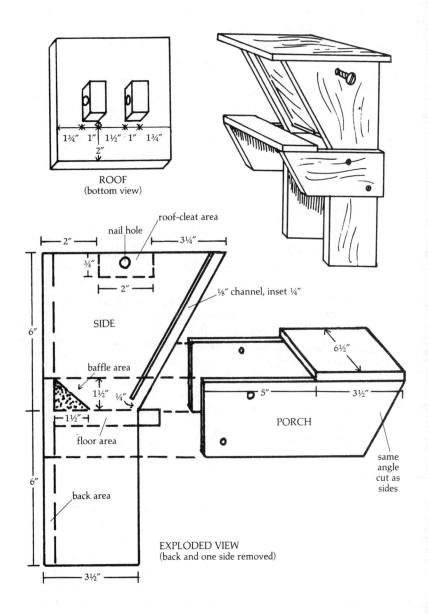

ROOF
(bottom view)

1¾" 1" 1½" 1" 1¾"
2"

roof-cleat area

nail hole

2" 3¼"

¾"

2"

⅛" channel, inset ¼"

SIDE

6"

6½"

baffle area

1½" ¼"

1½"

floor area

5" 3½"

PORCH

same
angle
cut as
sides

back area

6"

3½"

EXPLODED VIEW
(back and one side removed)

Fig. 19. Chickadee Feeder.

Construction Details

Materials   1″ × 4″ and 1″ × 8″ cedar;* ⅛″ glass; #8 × 1½″ wood
screws

	No. of Pieces	Dimensions
Seed-hopper roof	1	7″ × 7¼″ × ¾″
Roof cleats	2	2″ × 1″ × ¾″
Feeder sides	2	12″ × 7¼″ × ¾″
Back	1	12″ × 3½″ × ¾″
Seed baffle	1	2⅛″ × 3½″ × ¾″**
Glass insert	1	6⅝″ × 3¾″ × ⅛″
Floor	1	3½″ × 3½″ × ¾″
Porch roof	1	6½″ × 3½″ × ¾″
Porch sides	2	8½″ × 3½″ × ¾″
Porch fasteners	4	#8 1½″-long wood screw

*Actual dimensions ¾″ × 3½″ and ¾″ × 7¼″, respectively.
**Edges angle cut to fit flush against back and floor as shown in Fig. 19.

The height of the access space below can be adjusted as desired or the porch can be removed entirely to convert the design into that of a more conventional, albeit less restrictive, feeder. (For aesthetic balance the angle cut of the leading edge of the porch sides should match that of the feeder sides—about 60 degrees.) Finally, a baffle is used to channel seed to the exit opening of the seed hopper. Because of its small size it is best to lay the entire board from which it will be cut against one of the sides. Mark the angular-cut lines on the edges of the board and trim as required. (Using the baffle will require that the height of the seed exit be kept as narrow as possible without restricting seed flow. Otherwise seed will escape too rapidly and result in spilled waste. The ¼-inch height in the accompanying illustration is a useful guideline but some adjustment up or down may be required depending on the seed size contemplated.)

Squirrel-proof Feeder

This unconventional weight-activated feeder opens and closes automatically and is fully adjustable to limit seed access. In field trials cardinals, of medium weight, learned to alight gently with back-sweeping wings on a delicately balanced perch, gather seed, and fly to the top of the roof to hull and eat their bounty on more secure footing. Blue Jays, by their greater weight, were totally excluded from the shifting perch, as were other large birds and mammals, while smaller birds landed and fed at will, completely unperturbed. As a bonus, by removing the rotation-stop bar, refilling is a snap, as the roofed portion of the feeder sides can be rotated backward to reveal the entire seed-hopper area.

The actual details of construction are best understood when the feeder is viewed as two distinct parts: (1) the seed hopper and (2) the feeder shell, consisting of sides, roof, and supports. The seed hopper should be constructed first, as it is the nucleus, around which all other parts of the feeder will be based. Notice that the seed-hopper floor is actually 1⅝ inches shorter than the triangular sides. This difference provides a gap at the open back of the hopper which allows the sides to be slipped over the two-by-four upright and the whole hopper cocked downward in a later step. But first, locate the center hole in each side of the seed hopper by finding the midpoint of the longest side of each triangle (the side opposite the 90-degree angle). Draw a line from this mark back to the center of the 90-degree angle (or where the two shorter sides meet). Find the midpoint of this last line. This is the center point for the ⅜-inch bolt hole. Drill the hole and test-insert the ⅜-inch copper sleeves in each side. With the hopper sides, floor, roof (the roof should be set back 1½ inches from the outside edge of the hopper—the seed-stop end—to allow sufficient height for the seed-exit opening), and seed stop now attached, position the hopper against the two-by-four with the sides overlapping its edge. Tilt the hopper downward at least 20 degrees below horizontal to encourage gravity to draw seed in the hopper downward toward the seed exit. Before fastening, use a ruler to measure the distance from the center of the bolt hole to the top, back edge of the two-by-four support. This distance can be ½ to ¾ inch less than 6 inches (the radius of the 12-inch-diameter circle of the *feeder* sides) but should not approach the 6-inch limit. (Obviously the roof of the completed feeder might otherwise catch on the two-by-four during the course of its revolution or the perch might catch when the feeder is rotated back for filling. Conversely, however, the gap between two-by-four and roof should not be too great, or birds and animals might gain entrance over the back even with the feeder closed.) There should also be a ½-inch gap between the seed hopper and the outside edges of the feeder to allow

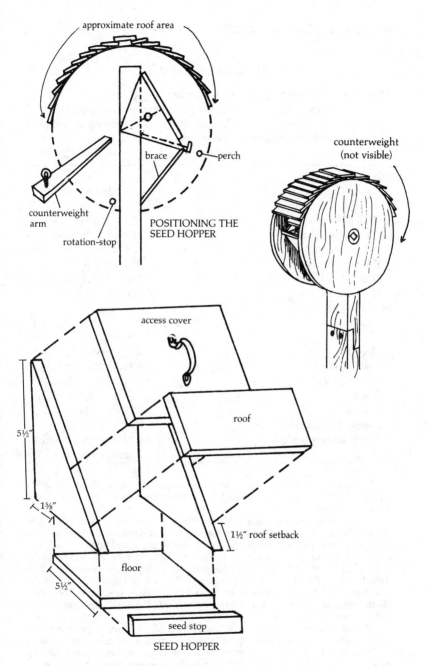

approximate roof area

brace

perch

counterweight arm

rotation-stop

POSITIONING THE SEED HOPPER

counterweight (not visible)

access cover

roof

5½"

1⅝"

1½" roof setback

floor

5½"

seed stop

SEED HOPPER

Fig. 20. Squirrel-proof Feeder.

Construction Details

Materials $^{19}\!/_{32}''$ and $^{3}\!/_{8}''$ plywood; $^{1}\!/_{8}''$ lumber; $2'' \times 4''$ lumber;* $^{1}\!/_{4}'' \times 2''$ cap bolts with nuts and washers; $^{3}\!/_{8}''$ copper water-supply tubing;** $^{1}\!/_{4}''$ hardwood dowel; eyebolt (for attachment of counterweights); galvanized sheet metal (optional)

	No. of Pieces	Dimensions
Feeder:		
Vertical support	1	$24'' \times 3^{1}\!/_{2}'' \times 1^{1}\!/_{2}''$
Sides	2	$12''$-dia. circle $\times$ $^{19}\!/_{32}''$
Roof pieces	18	$6^{1}\!/_{2}'' \times 1'' \times ^{1}\!/_{8}''$
Counterweight arm	1	$10^{1}\!/_{2}'' \times 2''$ (triangular) $\times ^{3}\!/_{8}''$
Seed-hopper brace	1	$7^{1}\!/_{2}'' \times 3^{1}\!/_{2}'' \times ^{3}\!/_{8}''$
Brace shield***	1	$7^{1}\!/_{2}'' \times 3^{1}\!/_{2}''$ sheet metal
Rotation-stop bar	1	$8^{1}\!/_{2}'' \times ^{1}\!/_{4}''$ dowel
Seed Hopper:		
Sides	2	$7^{1}\!/_{8}'' \times 5^{1}\!/_{2}''$ (triangular) $\times ^{19}\!/_{32}''$
Floor	1	$5^{1}\!/_{2}'' \times 3^{1}\!/_{2}'' \times ^{19}\!/_{32}''$
Roof section	1	$4^{11}\!/_{16}'' \times 2^{1}\!/_{4}'' \times ^{3}\!/_{8}''$
Access cover****	1	$4^{11}\!/_{16}'' \times 5'' \times ^{3}\!/_{8}''$
Perch	1	$6^{1}\!/_{2}'' \times ^{1}\!/_{4}''$ dowel
Seed stop	1	$3^{1}\!/_{2}'' \times 1'' \times ^{1}\!/_{8}''$
Copper bolt sleeve/spacer	2	$^{13}\!/_{16}'' \times ^{3}\!/_{8}''$ tubing
Cap bolts (cap screws)	2	$^{1}\!/_{4}'' \times 2''$ with nut and 3 washers per bolt

   *Actual dimensions $1^{1}\!/_{2}'' \times 3^{1}\!/_{2}''$.

   **Copper is a soft metal. Cut slowly, applying only moderate pressure, with a tubing cutter, hacksaw, or coping saw (with metal-cutting blade) to avoid deforming its circular shape.

   ***The shield, which is simply a thin sheet of metal covering the hopper brace, is optional. It helps to reduce sticking in the "tripped," or down, position, which may occur over time with repeated contact of the feeder perch and hopper brace. It is, however, only a minor inconvenience to reset the feeder. If a shield is desired, it may be attached directly to the face of the hopper brace with nails or screws (one or two should suffice). Even better, leave 1" tabs on either side of the shield at about the midpoint of each long side when first trimming to suggested dimensions. These tabs can then be bent over the back of the brace for support, allowing the shield to be easily added or removed as desired.

   ****Small birds may enter the seed hopper by climbing from the perch over the short hopper-roof section if their progress is not barred by the access cover. It need not be weathertight, nor does it need to be fastened down if in contact with the top edge of the hopper roof. A small handle or finger holes will greatly assist in its removal and replacement.

clearance for installing the perch. Fasten the seed hopper to the two-by-four and add the seed-hopper brace for extra strength and support.

For the final phase of construction, bore center holes in the two feeder sides. (The holes must be sized for the cap bolts but are not required to accommodate the copper sleeves.) Test-fit the sides by (1) inserting the copper sleeves into the hopper holes (any excess length should extend outward toward the feeder sides), (2) inserting a washer over each bolt, (3) inserting the bolts through the feeder sides and adding a second washer, and (4) inserting the bolts through the copper sleeves and adding a final washer and nut (do not overtighten—freedom of movement is essential). Test movement. Disassemble and attach overlapping roof sections. (They should cover an arc from approximately nine o'clock to two o'clock. To test, the seed hopper should be completely covered when the feeder is in the closed position, with no gaps near the two-by-four to allow entry. In the refill position, with the rotation-stop removed, there should be ample access to the seed-hopper area as well.) Attach the counterweight arm to the exterior of one feeder side at a downward angle of about 50 degrees, or approximately the eight-o'clock position. It should extend roughly 4¾ inches beyond the rim of the feeder side. Attach the eyebolt at a convenient point on this extended portion near its outside edge. Reassemble the feeder. Position the roofed section so that there is sufficient allowance for seed access when the feeder is in the up, or open, position. Mark the position of the perch (ideally it should be just above the level of the seed stop to force any animal or bird to contact it before reaching the seed opening). Mark the position of the rotation-stop (against the back edge of and in contact with the two-by-four). Note that the rotation-stop bar will extend outward—its excess length acting as a handle, or hand grip. Install the perch and rotation-stop dowels.

Now the feeder should only rotate forward and come to a stop when the perch contacts the seed-hopper brace. The two-by-four upright can be mounted on a suitable support as desired. Because the counterweight arm, the eyebolt, and the excess number of roof sections on the back side of the feeder all add weight to that side, it may not be necessary to add additional weight to counterbalance the weight of smaller birds landing on the perch. If more weight is desired, lead fishing sinkers (some with brass eyelets for easy attachment) can be obtained at any sporting-goods store in fractional and whole ounces, or small quantities of pebbles, sand, etc., can be suspended from the eyebolt in a small bag or cup. If the counterweight should already appear to be too heavy for your goal (the perch weight at which you wish the feeder to close) without the addition of any more weight, simply add weights to the outside of the opposite, or seed-hopper-opening, side of the feeder to compensate. Finally, because motion will eventually loosen the retaining nuts, they should be periodically hand-tightened during refill operations.

V. Final Placement

General Site Selection and Mounting

Once a feeder is ready to be placed in service, careful consideration should be given to its location. Ideally it should be in clear view from some convenient window of your home. It should be easily accessible for refilling in inclement weather—near a walk or garden path for example. Birds also will feel more at ease if feeders are within quick flying distance of cover since the Sharp-shinned Hawk and some other hawks, shrikes, and free-roaming cats may prey on small birds. Cats, in particular, may lurk in the shadows of low shrubbery waiting for a chance to charge and pounce, so be sure to allow an open area around ground-level feeders for early warning and escape. If possible, keep the feeders at least eight feet from tall trees or utility poles and fences from which squirrels can leap. If you are familiar with the local weather conditions you may want to place feeder openings away from the direction of prevailing winds (for instance, in much of North America severe winter storms tend to arrive from the north and west).

Hanging feeders should not be wired directly to trees, as the friction of movement and the natural growth of the supporting limb will eventually cause injury. Instead, cover the wire with an old piece of garden hose or hang the feeder from a crossbar, pole, or other artificial device. Remember, too, that eyebolts rather than screweyes are the preferred means of attachment for hanging-feeder wires or cords, as there is much less risk that they will pull out of the wood over time.

For maximum protection and security, post feeders are best mounted at least five feet high whenever possible and convenient.

Fig. 21. Mobile feeder stand (bottom).

The feeders themselves are generally so light that supporting posts need not be set more than 18–24 inches in the ground when permanently installed, and concrete anchors or crossbracing is rarely recommended. Portable supports (Fig. 21) in a variety of styles allow feeders to be moved about with the seasons.

Pest guards (See Figs. 4 and 5, Chapter I) are almost mandatory in some locations and with some foods and feeder styles. Tim Williams of the Clyde E. Buckley Wildlife Sanctuary mentions, in addition to the already noted problem animals, that raccoons and even voles will raid feeders in his rural location.[19] For the average backyard feeding station, however, the possible competitors are both less numerous and less demanding and persistent.

---

[19]Tim Williams, Manager/Naturalist, Clyde E. Buckley Wildlife Sanctuary, Frankfort, Ky., personal communication with author, 27 October 1987.

Suet feeders present a special problem of their own, as two of their primary users, woodpeckers and creepers, spend much of their time searching tree bark for hidden food. Woodpeckers in particular will eventually find suet no matter where it is placed, but it is always more effective to place it in or near a fencerow or other area where there are mature trees. The feeders may be attached to the bark itself, suspended from a limb, or even supported on a nearby pole or fence post.

Because empty seed hulls are typically small and readily decay they do not usually cause buildup problems. Feeders over paved areas should be avoided. If you are one of the lucky few with a yard that is more golf green than lawn you may wish to install your feeders in or over flower beds, ground cover, or garden spaces. Less desirable but reasonably effective are detachable trays or other devices to catch falling debris.

Seasonal Feeding Requirements

Many bird lovers feed birds the year round, while others follow a strict regimen from Labor Day, or early September, to June. Each season has its special joys. Clearly birds are less dependent on help in summer, with bountiful natural sources of supply easily available— some of which, e.g., fresh fruit, may even, temporarily at least, be more attractive than our own offerings. Yet few sights are more endearing than a mother bird feeding her brood or a whole family group descending at once on a feeder. Summer feeding stations may also provide the only opportunities for viewing some migratory species that may winter thousands of miles to the south. In winter the need for supplemental food is much greater in northern latitudes. Days are shorter, allowing less time for food search, snow and ice storms may make natural foods inaccessible, and low temperatures combined with long nights increase energy requirements. The greatest need of all may be in springtime when many wild seed supplies have already been gleaned for months by local birds, fresh food sources have not yet matured, changeable weather patterns cause unpredictable late storms, and migration and breeding pressures bring hungry new arrivals into unfamiliar feeding territories.

Authorities are divided about the effects of stopping a feeding program once it has begun. It is doubtful that small-scale efforts cause much disruption when discontinued, as birds will simply move on to other sources. Large-scale feeding programs that offer large amounts of multiple varieties of seed and attract dozens if not hundreds of birds each day should probably be tapered off gradually to allow larger flocks to disperse. If at all possible, avoid terminating a feeding program in late winter or early spring.

Feeder Discovery Periods

Once a feeder is in place, it can take as little as twenty-four hours for local birds to begin using it. This is especially true if other feeders are already in use—either your own or a neighbor's close by. Birds are rightfully cautious and suspicious of new things and it will more typically take four or five days. More complicated designs, especially some of the species-restrictive styles, may require several weeks. (Obviously the species for which it is intended must frequent your area—a fact that cannot always be established until after the feeder is placed in service.) Suet feeders are the slowest to attract interest because birds such as woodpeckers, prime suet users, are solitary individuals in winter traveling a large area in search of over-wintering insect larvae. If they are not accustomed to finding suet or sampling corn or hulled sunflower at your feeding station, it can take weeks to a month or longer for discovery. Check the suet from time to time. Woodpeckers arrive quietly. Your first awareness of their presence will likely be numerous small peck holes. Once these are discovered you can begin actively watching. Believe me. It is worth the wait. Few birds stir the imagination and thrill the heart as a woodpecker does when it appears unexpectedly at a suburban feeder for the very first time. The following is an excerpt from a personal journal describing an incident involving a new suet feeder placed in service in an average suburban yard nearly a full month before:

> Thursday, February 19 . . . Suet feeders seem to be a bust in present locations and will have to be moved. WOW! Scarcely an hour after making the previous observation I discovered the female Downy Woodpecker clinging tenaciously upside-down on one of the hanging, medallion-style suet feeders.

Even now as I write this, many months later, I can still recall the excitement and wonder of that special moment. "WOW!" does indeed sum it up nicely.

Storing Seed and General Yearly Maintenance

If seed is purchased in bulk it should be stored in a cool, dry area. Hulled or milled seeds like sunflower chips, peanut hearts, or cracked corn are more susceptible to deterioration and should be kept in plastic bags or airtight containers. Small amounts can be kept in clean plastic milk jugs. Large amounts of all types of seed are best kept in large plastic or galvanized trash cans with tight-fitting lids to avoid attracting rodents or other pests.

Weevil eggs are present in many seeds. After several weeks of warm temperatures they may hatch and mature into small, beetle-like adults. Obviously seed quality will suffer, although you may continue to distribute old seed until supplies are exhausted. But it is better to purchase more frequently and in smaller quantities over the warm-weather months. Dwight M. Brown of Geo. W. Hill & Co., a large regional supplier of wild-bird seed, informs me that their seed is kept in cool storage to insure high quality right up to the moment of shipment.[20] It is therefore safe to assume that seed purchased from reputable suppliers should last for many weeks without deterioration and, if properly stored, for six months or longer on average. Naturally, contaminated containers should be cleaned before adding fresh seed.

Suet will keep indefinitely out-of-doors in cool weather. Once the weather warms, some melting and eventual discoloration may occur, and smaller portions should then be used and discarded more frequently. Excess suet may be frozen in individual serving sizes appropriate for your needs.

To keep small problems from becoming big ones, feeders should be checked twice yearly, spring and fall, for weather damage. Motion feeders like the weathervane and some squirrel-proof designs may require lubrication, bolt tightening, or other minor adjustments. Hopper glass should be cleaned as well. Depending on manufacturers' recommendations, the finish (whether paint, sealer, or stain) should be recoated every two or three years. I suggest that you keep one or two feeders in reserve. While one feeder is being cleaned or repaired there will always be a stand-in to take its place, assuring uninterrupted feeding routines.

---

[20]Dwight M. Brown, Geo. W. Hill & Co., Inc., personal communication with author, 1 September 1987.

VI. IN CLOSING

Food is the essential ingredient in the well-being of all birds. As mentioned earlier, providing it is the fastest and most direct method of aiding avian wildlife. As with man, however, food alone will not furnish all the necessary elements of a well-rounded program to support and provide care.

Water, vital for all life processes, is a close second to food in importance. Birds also bathe for parasite control and feather maintenance. Open, accessible water in shallow containers is a real boon in northern climes where normal sources of water are frozen over or many miles distant in winter. Water in motion in an ornamental pool or trickling from a higher elevation seems to hold a particular fascination. At times, especially in more arid parts of the country, water may be an even more compelling attraction than food.

The importance of shelter for protection from predators has already been touched upon. Shelter in the form of trees or shrubs also shields against ice, rain, snow, cold winter wind, or hot summer sunshine. Trees and shrubs provide places for roosting at night and secluded retreats for calm repose by day.

Closely allied with the need for shelter is that for nest sites. For many species, living plants are the answer, but for a small but significant minority of birds, including the Eastern Bluebird, only large, enclosed cavities, like those made by woodpeckers in dead or dying trees, will do. With today's modern, "clean" cultivation, dead trees, or snags, are not left standing, injured trees are trimmed of dead wood, and large wooden fenceposts, which once provided homes for many small birds in rural areas, are rapidly being replaced by metal. These birds, "cavity nesters," as they are called, will accept man-made boxes that approximate natural conditions in the wild. A box 5 inches square inside and 8 inches deep, with a 1½-inch entrance hole 6 inches above the floor and mounted 10 feet high, should attract several species. For more specific requirements and a complete list of cavity nesters, consult various texts listed in the bibliography of this book or the author's own *The Complete Book of Birdhouse Construction for Woodworkers*, also published by Dover Publications, Inc. (24407-5). Similarly, old birdhouses and special roost boxes can serve as winter shelter in northern latitudes.

Some Planting Suggestions

Shelter, nest sites, and even food can be provided by the judicious use of plantings. The following regionalized tables are based on helpful summaries provided by the Soil Conservation Service of the U.S. Department of Agriculture (consult your local nurseryman for availability and planting suggestions).

TABLE 5
Wildlife Plantings—Northeast[21]

Plant	Growth Habit	Bird Species Attracted
Trees		
Crabapple (*Malus* spp.)	small tree	18
Holly (*Ilex* spp.)	shrub to tree	22
Flowering Dogwood (*Cornus florida*)	large shrub to small tree	36
Cherry (*Prunus* spp.)	shrub to large tree	40
Mountain Ash (*Sorbus* spp.)	shrub to medium tree	15
Hawthorn (*Crataegus* spp.)	small tree	25
Red Cedar (*Juniperus virginiana*)	shrub to medium tree	68
Shrubs		
Amur Honeysuckle (*Lonicera Maackii*)	large shrub	8
Firethorn (*Pyracantha* spp.)	medium shrub	17
Autumn Olive (*Elaeagnus umbellata*)	large, spreading shrub	25
Silky Dogwood (*Cornus Amomum*)	medium shrub	10
Highbush Blueberry (*Vaccinium corymbosum*)	medium shrub	36
Sumac (*Rhus* spp.)	medium to large shrub	17
Panicled (Gray) Dogwood (*Cornus racemosa*)	thicket-forming medium shrub	16
American Highbush Cranberry (*Viburnum trilobum*)	upright, tall shrub	34
Red-osier Dogwood (*Cornus sericea*)	medium shrub	19
Tatarian Honeysuckle (*Lonicera tatarica*)	medium shrub	17
Vines		
American Bittersweet (*Celastrus scandens*)	twining vine	10
Virginia Creeper (*Parthenocissus quinquefolia*)	ground or climbing vine	37

[21]U.S. Department of Agriculture, Soil Conservation Service, *Invite Birds to Your Home: Conservation Plantings for the Northeast* (Washington, D.C.: U.S. Government Printing Office, 1969), no pagination, see specific entries.

TABLE 6
Wildlife Plantings—Northwest[22]

Plant	Growth Habit	Bird Species Attracted
Trees		
Hawthorn (*Crataegus* spp.)	small tree	23
Mountain Ash (*Sorbus* spp.)	medium tree	21
Buckthorn (*Rhamnus* spp.)	large shrub to small tree	19
Crabapple (*Malus* spp.)	small tree	33
Wild Cherry (*Prunus* spp.)	shrub to small tree	44
Dogwood (*Cornus* spp.)	shrub to tree	41
Holly (*Ilex* spp.)	shrub to tree	24
Russian Olive (*Elaeagnus angustifolia*)	large shrub to small tree	20
Domestic Cherry (*Prunus* spp.)	shrub to large tree	37
Juniper (*Juniperus* spp.)	shrub to tree	30
Serviceberry (*Amelanchier* spp.)	shrub to small tree	31
Shrubs		
Snowberry (*Symphoricarpos* spp.)	small shrub	19
Firethorn (*Pyracantha* spp.)	medium shrub	16
Currants & Gooseberries (*Ribes* spp.)	small to medium shrub	23
Cotoneaster (*Cotoneaster* spp.)	small to medium shrub	10
Oregon Grape (*Mahonia* spp.)	small shrub	37
Blackberry & Raspberry (*Rubus* spp.)	small to medium shrub (thornless varieties available)	50
Elderberry (*Sambucus* spp.)	tall shrub to tree	62

[22][L. Dean Marriage], U.S. Department of Agriculture, Soil Conservation Service, *Invite Birds to Your Home: Conservation Plantings for the Northwest* (Washington, D.C.: U.S. Government Printing Office, 1975), pp. 14–19.

TABLE 7
Wildlife Plantings—Midwest[23]

Plant	Growth Habit	Bird Species Attracted
Trees		
Cherry (*Prunus* spp)	shrub to large tree	49
Wild Plum (*Prunus americana*)	shrub to small tree	16
Dogwood (*Cornus* spp.)	small shrub to small tree	47
Mountain Ash (*Sorbus* spp.)	medium tree	20
Russian Olive (*Elaeagnus angustifolia*)	large shrub to small tree	31
Red Cedar (*Juniperus virginiana*)	shrub to medium tree	25
Crabapple (*Malus* spp.)	small tree	29
Holly (*Ilex* spp.)	shrub to tree	20
Hawthorn (*Crataegus* spp.)	small tree	19
Shrubs		
Autumn Olive (*Elaeagnus umbellata*)	large, spreading shrub	15
Cotoneaster (*Cotoneaster* spp.)	small to medium shrub	6
Tatarian Honeysuckle (*Lonicera tatarica*)	medium shrub	18
Firethorn (*Pyracantha* spp.)	medium shrub	17
Elderberry (*Sambucus* spp.)	tall shrub to tree	50
American Highbush Cranberry (*Viburnum trilobum*)	upright, tall shrub	28
Vine		
American Bittersweet (*Celastrus scandens*)	twining vine	12

23[Wade H. Hamor], U.S. Department of Agriculture, Soil Conservation Service, *Invite Birds to Your Home: Conservation Plantings for the Midwest* (Washington, D.C.: U.S. Government Printing Office, 1971), no pagination, see specific entries.

TABLE 8
Wildlife Plantings—Southeast[24]

Plant	Growth Habit	Bird Species Attracted
Trees		
Crabapple (*Malus* spp.)	small tree	24
Sawtooth Oak (*Quercus acutissima*)	large tree	37
Hawthorn (*Crataegus* spp.)	small tree	19
Holly (*Ilex* spp.)	shrub to tree	28
Flowering Dogwood (*Cornus florida*)	shrub to small tree	45
Wild Plum (*Prunus americana*)	shrub to small tree	16
Cherry (*Prunus* spp.)	shrub to large tree	47
Red Cedar (*Juniperus virginiana*)	shrub to medium tree	22
Shrubs		
Sumac (*Rhus* spp.)	medium to large shrub	36
Firethorn (*Pyracantha* spp.)	medium shrub	16
Elderberry (*Sambucus* spp.)	tall shrub to tree	51
American Beautyberry (*Callicarpa americana*)	medium shrub	12
Nandina (*Nandina domestica*)	medium shrub	12
Amur Honeysuckle (*Lonicera Maackii*)	large shrub	19
Autumn Olive (*Elaeagnus umbellata*)	large, spreading shrub	25
Thorny Elaeagnus (*Elaeagnus pungens*)	tall shrub	9
Vine		
Maypop Passionflower (*Passiflora incarnata*)	climbing vine	10

[24][Olan W. Dillon, Jr.], U.S. Department of Agriculture, Soil Conservation Service, *Invite Birds to Your Home: Conservation Plantings for the Southeast* (Washington, D.C.: U.S. Government Printing Office, 1975), pp. 8–13.

TABLE 9
Some Popular Hummingbird Flowers*

Azalea	Lily—both Tiger lily & Daylily
Bee balm or Monarda	Locust
Balsam or Touch-me-not	Lupine
Buddleia or Butterfly bush	Mimosa or Silk tree
Canna	Morning-glory
Cardinal flower or Scarlet lobelia	Nicotiana (Flowering or Ornamental Tobacco)
Cleome or Spider plant	
Columbine	Penstemon or Beard-tongue
Coralbells	Petunia
Fuchsia	Flowering quince
Geranium	Salvia or Scarlet sage
Scarlet gilia	Scabiosa
Honeysuckle	Weigela or Cardinal shrub
Scarlet larkspur	Zinnia

*Where different color varieties of the same flower are available, bright reds are preferred. This list is not exhaustive. Check with your local nurseryman for availability and hardiness as well as for other planting suggestions.

BIBLIOGRAPHY

Bard, Rachel. *Successful Wood Book: How to Choose, Use, and Finish Every Kind of Wood.* Farmington, Mich.: Structures Publishing Company, 1978.

Bent, Arthur Cleveland [and Collaborators]. *Life Histories of North American Cardinals, Grosbeaks, Buntings, Towhees, Finches, Sparrows, and Allies.* Part One. Reprint. New York: Dover Publications, Inc., 1968.

Bent, Arthur Cleveland. *Life Histories of North American Cuckoos, Goatsuckers, Hummingbirds and Their Allies.* Reprint. New York: Dover Publications, Inc., 1964, 1989.

Bull, John, and John Farrand, Jr. *The Audubon Society Field Guide to North American Birds: Eastern Region.* N.Y.: Alfred A. Knopf, 1977.

[Dillon, Olan W., Jr.] U.S. Department of Agriculture. Soil Conservation Service. *Invite Birds to Your Home: Conservation Plantings for the Southeast.* Washington, D.C.: U.S. Government Printing Office, 1975.

Forest Products Laboratory. *Wood Handbook: Wood as an Engineering Material.* U.S.D.A. Agriculture Handbook No. 72. Rev. ed. Washington, D.C.: U.S. Government Printing Office, 1974.

Geis, Aelred D., and Donald B. Hyde, Jr. *Wild Bird Feeding Preferences: A Guide to the Most Attractive Bird Foods.* Washington, D.C.: National Wildlife Federation, 1983.

Geis, Aelred D. *Relative Attractiveness of Different Foods at Wild Bird Feeders.* Special Scientific Report—Wildlife No. 233. U.S. Department of the Interior. Fish and Wildlife Service. Washington, D.C.: U.S. Government Printing Office, 1980.

Grant, Karen A., and Verne Grant. *Hummingbirds and Their Flowers.* N.Y.: Columbia University Press, 1968.

Hammond, James J., *et al. Woodworking Technology.* Bloomington, Illinois: McKnight & McKnight Publishing Company, 1961.

[Hamor, Wade H.] U.S. Department of Agriculture. Soil Conservation Service. *Invite Birds to Your Home: Conservation Plantings for the Midwest.* Washington, D.C.: U.S. Government Printing Office, 1971.

Harrison, George H. *The Backyard Bird Watcher*. N.Y.: Simon and Schuster, 1979.

Holmgren, Virginia C. *The Way of the Hummingbird: In Legend, History and Today's Gardens*. Santa Barbara, Cal.: Capra Press, 1986.

Kircher, John C. "Feeding the Life List." *Bird Watcher's Digest* 4, No. 3 (1982), 72–79.

Klamkin, Charles. *Weather Vanes: The History, Design, and Manufacture of an American Folk Art*. N.Y.: Hawthorn Books, Inc., 1973.

Klein, Stanley. *The Encyclopedia of North American Wildlife*. N.Y.: Facts on File, Inc., 1983.

Lowe's 1974 Buyers Guide. North Wilkesboro, N.C.: Lowe's Companies, Inc., 1974.

McElroy, Thomas P., Jr. *Handbook of Attracting Birds*. N.Y.: Alfred A. Knopf, 1950.

———. *The New Handbook of Attracting Birds*. 2d ed. N.Y.: Alfred A. Knopf, 1969.

McKenny, Margaret. *Birds in the Garden and How to Attract Them*. N.Y.: Grosset & Dunlap, 1939.

[Marriage, L. Dean.] U.S. Department of Agriculture. Soil Conservation Service. *Invite Birds to Your Home: Conservation Plantings for the Northwest*. Washington, D.C.: U.S. Government Printing Office, 1975.

Miller, Richard S., and Richard Elton Miller. "Feeding Activity and Color Preference of Ruby-throated Hummingbirds." *The Condor* 73, No. 3 (1971), 309–13.

Robbins, Chandler S., Bertel Bruun, and Herbert S. Zim. *Birds of North America: A Guide to Field Identification*. N.Y.: Golden Press, 1966.

Skutch, Alexander F. *The Life of the Hummingbird*. N.Y.: Crown Publishers, Inc., 1973.

Terres, John K. *The Audubon Society Encyclopedia of North American Birds*. N.Y.: Alfred A. Knopf, 1980.

———. *Songbirds in Your Garden*. N.Y.: Thomas Y. Crowell Company, 1953.

Udvardy, Miklos D. F. *The Audubon Society Field Guide to North American Birds: Western Region*. N.Y.: Alfred A. Knopf, 1977.

U.S. Department of Agriculture. Soil Conservation Service. *Invite Birds to Your Home: Conservation Plantings for the Northeast*. Washington, D.C.: U.S. Government Printing Office, 1969.

A CATALOG OF SELECTED
DOVER BOOKS
IN ALL FIELDS OF INTEREST

A CATALOG OF SELECTED DOVER
BOOKS IN ALL FIELDS OF INTEREST

CONCERNING THE SPIRITUAL IN ART, Wassily Kandinsky. Pioneering work by father of abstract art. Thoughts on color theory, nature of art. Analysis of earlier masters. 12 illustrations. 80pp. of text. 5⅜ x 8½. 0-486-23411-8

CELTIC ART: The Methods of Construction, George Bain. Simple geometric techniques for making Celtic interlacements, spirals, Kells-type initials, animals, humans, etc. Over 500 illustrations. 160pp. 9 x 12. (Available in U.S. only.) 0-486-22923-8

AN ATLAS OF ANATOMY FOR ARTISTS, Fritz Schider. Most thorough reference work on art anatomy in the world. Hundreds of illustrations, including selections from works by Vesalius, Leonardo, Goya, Ingres, Michelangelo, others. 593 illustrations. 192pp. 7⅛ x 10¼. 0-486-20241-0

CELTIC HAND STROKE-BY-STROKE (Irish Half-Uncial from "The Book of Kells"): An Arthur Baker Calligraphy Manual, Arthur Baker. Complete guide to creating each letter of the alphabet in distinctive Celtic manner. Covers hand position, strokes, pens, inks, paper, more. Illustrated. 48pp. 8¼ x 11. 0-486-24336-2

EASY ORIGAMI, John Montroll. Charming collection of 32 projects (hat, cup, pelican, piano, swan, many more) specially designed for the novice origami hobbyist. Clearly illustrated easy-to-follow instructions insure that even beginning papercrafters will achieve successful results. 48pp. 8¼ x 11. 0-486-27298-2

BLOOMINGDALE'S ILLUSTRATED 1886 CATALOG: Fashions, Dry Goods and Housewares, Bloomingdale Brothers. Famed merchants' extremely rare catalog depicting about 1,700 products: clothing, housewares, firearms, dry goods, jewelry, more. Invaluable for dating, identifying vintage items. Also, copyright-free graphics for artists, designers. Co-published with Henry Ford Museum & Greenfield Village. 160pp. 8¼ x 11. 0-486-25780-0

THE ART OF WORLDLY WISDOM, Baltasar Gracian. "Think with the few and speak with the many," "Friends are a second existence," and "Be able to forget" are among this 1637 volume's 300 pithy maxims. A perfect source of mental and spiritual refreshment, it can be opened at random and appreciated either in brief or at length. 128pp. 5⅜ x 8½. 0-486-44034-6

JOHNSON'S DICTIONARY: A Modern Selection, Samuel Johnson (E. L. McAdam and George Milne, eds.). This modern version reduces the original 1755 edition's 2,300 pages of definitions and literary examples to a more manageable length, retaining the verbal pleasure and historical curiosity of the original. 480pp. 5³⁄₁₆ x 8¼. 0-486-44089-3

ADVENTURES OF HUCKLEBERRY FINN, Mark Twain, Illustrated by E. W. Kemble. A work of eternal richness and complexity, a source of ongoing critical debate, and a literary landmark, Twain's 1885 masterpiece about a barefoot boy's journey of self-discovery has enthralled readers around the world. This handsome clothbound reproduction of the first edition features all 174 of the original black-and-white illustrations. 368pp. 5⅜ x 8½. 0-486-44322-1

STICKLEY CRAFTSMAN FURNITURE CATALOGS, Gustav Stickley and L. & J. G. Stickley. Beautiful, functional furniture in two authentic catalogs from 1910. 594 illustrations, including 277 photos, show settles, rockers, armchairs, reclining chairs, bookcases, desks, tables. 183pp. 6½ x 9¼. 0-486-23838-5

AMERICAN LOCOMOTIVES IN HISTORIC PHOTOGRAPHS: 1858 to 1949, Ron Ziel (ed.). A rare collection of 126 meticulously detailed official photographs, called "builder portraits," of American locomotives that majestically chronicle the rise of steam locomotive power in America. Introduction. Detailed captions. xi+ 129pp. 9 x 12. 0-486-27393-8

AMERICA'S LIGHTHOUSES: An Illustrated History, Francis Ross Holland, Jr. Delightfully written, profusely illustrated fact-filled survey of over 200 American lighthouses since 1716. History, anecdotes, technological advances, more. 240pp. 8 x 10¾. 0-486-25576-X

TOWARDS A NEW ARCHITECTURE, Le Corbusier. Pioneering manifesto by founder of "International School." Technical and aesthetic theories, views of industry, economics, relation of form to function, "mass-production split" and much more. Profusely illustrated. 320pp. 6⅛ x 9¼. (Available in U.S. only.) 0-486-25023-7

HOW THE OTHER HALF LIVES, Jacob Riis. Famous journalistic record, exposing poverty and degradation of New York slums around 1900, by major social reformer. 100 striking and influential photographs. 233pp. 10 x 7⅞. 0-486-22012-5

FRUIT KEY AND TWIG KEY TO TREES AND SHRUBS, William M. Harlow. One of the handiest and most widely used identification aids. Fruit key covers 120 deciduous and evergreen species; twig key 160 deciduous species. Easily used. Over 300 photographs. 126pp. 5⅜ x 8½. 0-486-20511-8

COMMON BIRD SONGS, Dr. Donald J. Borror. Songs of 60 most common U.S. birds: robins, sparrows, cardinals, bluejays, finches, more–arranged in order of increasing complexity. Up to 9 variations of songs of each species.
Cassette and manual 0-486-99911-4

ORCHIDS AS HOUSE PLANTS, Rebecca Tyson Northen. Grow cattleyas and many other kinds of orchids–in a window, in a case, or under artificial light. 63 illustrations. 148pp. 5⅜ x 8½. 0-486-23261-1

MONSTER MAZES, Dave Phillips. Masterful mazes at four levels of difficulty. Avoid deadly perils and evil creatures to find magical treasures. Solutions for all 32 exciting illustrated puzzles. 48pp. 8¼ x 11. 0-486-26005-4

MOZART'S DON GIOVANNI (DOVER OPERA LIBRETTO SERIES), Wolfgang Amadeus Mozart. Introduced and translated by Ellen H. Bleiler. Standard Italian libretto, with complete English translation. Convenient and thoroughly portable–an ideal companion for reading along with a recording or the performance itself. Introduction. List of characters. Plot summary. 121pp. 5¼ x 8½. 0-486-24944-1

FRANK LLOYD WRIGHT'S DANA HOUSE, Donald Hoffmann. Pictorial essay of residential masterpiece with over 160 interior and exterior photos, plans, elevations, sketches and studies. 128pp. 9¼ x 10¾. 0-486-29120-0

PSYCHOLOGY OF MUSIC, Carl E. Seashore. Classic work discusses music as a medium from psychological viewpoint. Clear treatment of physical acoustics, auditory apparatus, sound perception, development of musical skills, nature of musical feeling, host of other topics. 88 figures. 408pp. 5⅜ x 8½.   0-486-21851-1

LIFE IN ANCIENT EGYPT, Adolf Erman. Fullest, most thorough, detailed older account with much not in more recent books, domestic life, religion, magic, medicine, commerce, much more. Many illustrations reproduce tomb paintings, carvings, hieroglyphs, etc. 597pp. 5⅜ x 8½.   0-486-22632-8

SUNDIALS, Their Theory and Construction, Albert Waugh. Far and away the best, most thorough coverage of ideas, mathematics concerned, types, construction, adjusting anywhere. Simple, nontechnical treatment allows even children to build several of these dials. Over 100 illustrations. 230pp. 5⅜ x 8½.   0-486-22947-5

THEORETICAL HYDRODYNAMICS, L. M. Milne-Thomson. Classic exposition of the mathematical theory of fluid motion, applicable to both hydrodynamics and aerodynamics. Over 600 exercises. 768pp. 6⅛ x 9¼.   0-486-68970-0

OLD-TIME VIGNETTES IN FULL COLOR, Carol Belanger Grafton (ed.). Over 390 charming, often sentimental illustrations, selected from archives of Victorian graphics—pretty women posing, children playing, food, flowers, kittens and puppies, smiling cherubs, birds and butterflies, much more. All copyright-free. 48pp. 9¼ x 12¼.
0-486-27269-9

PERSPECTIVE FOR ARTISTS, Rex Vicat Cole. Depth, perspective of sky and sea, shadows, much more, not usually covered. 391 diagrams, 81 reproductions of drawings and paintings. 279pp. 5⅜ x 8½.   0-486-22487-2

DRAWING THE LIVING FIGURE, Joseph Sheppard. Innovative approach to artistic anatomy focuses on specifics of surface anatomy, rather than muscles and bones. Over 170 drawings of live models in front, back and side views, and in widely varying poses. Accompanying diagrams. 177 illustrations. Introduction. Index. 144pp. 8⅜ x11¼.   0-486-26723-7

GOTHIC AND OLD ENGLISH ALPHABETS: 100 Complete Fonts, Dan X. Solo. Add power, elegance to posters, signs, other graphics with 100 stunning copyright-free alphabets: Blackstone, Dolbey, Germania, 97 more—including many lower-case, numerals, punctuation marks. 104pp. 8⅛ x 11.   0-486-24695-7

THE BOOK OF WOOD CARVING, Charles Marshall Sayers. Finest book for beginners discusses fundamentals and offers 34 designs. "Absolutely first rate . . . well thought out and well executed."–E. J. Tangerman. 118pp. 7¾ x 10⅝.   0-486-23654-4

ILLUSTRATED CATALOG OF CIVIL WAR MILITARY GOODS: Union Army Weapons, Insignia, Uniform Accessories, and Other Equipment, Schuyler, Hartley, and Graham. Rare, profusely illustrated 1846 catalog includes Union Army uniform and dress regulations, arms and ammunition, coats, insignia, flags, swords, rifles, etc. 226 illustrations. 160pp. 9 x 12.   0-486-24939-5

WOMEN'S FASHIONS OF THE EARLY 1900s: An Unabridged Republication of "New York Fashions, 1909," National Cloak & Suit Co. Rare catalog of mail-order fashions documents women's and children's clothing styles shortly after the turn of the century. Captions offer full descriptions, prices. Invaluable resource for fashion, costume historians. Approximately 725 illustrations. 128pp. 8⅜ x 11¼.
0-486-27276-1

HOW TO DO BEADWORK, Mary White. Fundamental book on craft from simple projects to five-bead chains and woven works. 106 illustrations. 142pp. 5⅜ x 8.
0-486-20697-1

THE 1912 AND 1915 GUSTAV STICKLEY FURNITURE CATALOGS, Gustav Stickley. With over 200 detailed illustrations and descriptions, these two catalogs are essential reading and reference materials and identification guides for Stickley furniture. Captions cite materials, dimensions and prices. 112pp. 6½ x 9¼. 0-486-26676-1

EARLY AMERICAN LOCOMOTIVES, John H. White, Jr. Finest locomotive engravings from early 19th century: historical (1804–74), main-line (after 1870), special, foreign, etc. 147 plates. 142pp. 11⅜ x 8¼. 0-486-22772-3

LITTLE BOOK OF EARLY AMERICAN CRAFTS AND TRADES, Peter Stockham (ed.). 1807 children's book explains crafts and trades: baker, hatter, cooper, potter, and many others. 23 copperplate illustrations. 140pp. 4⅝ x 6.
0-486-23336-7

VICTORIAN FASHIONS AND COSTUMES FROM HARPER'S BAZAR, 1867–1898, Stella Blum (ed.). Day costumes, evening wear, sports clothes, shoes, hats, other accessories in over 1,000 detailed engravings. 320pp. 9⅜ x 12¼.
0-486-22990-4

THE LONG ISLAND RAIL ROAD IN EARLY PHOTOGRAPHS, Ron Ziel. Over 220 rare photos, informative text document origin (· 1844) and development of rail service on Long Island. Vintage views of early trains, locomotives, stations, passengers, crews, much more. Captions. 8⅞ x 11¾. 0-486-26301-0

VOYAGE OF THE LIBERDADE, Joshua Slocum. Great 19th-century mariner's thrilling, first-hand account of the wreck of his ship off South America, the 35-foot boat he built from the wreckage, and its remarkable voyage home. 128pp. 5⅜ x 8½.
0-486-40022-0

TEN BOOKS ON ARCHITECTURE, Vitruvius. The most important book ever written on architecture. Early Roman aesthetics, technology, classical orders, site selection, all other aspects. Morgan translation. 331pp. 5⅜ x 8½. 0-486-20645-9

THE HUMAN FIGURE IN MOTION, Eadweard Muybridge. More than 4,500 stopped-action photos, in action series, showing undraped men, women, children jumping, lying down, throwing, sitting, wrestling, carrying, etc. 390pp. 7⅞ x 10⅝.
0-486-20204-6 Clothbd.

TREES OF THE EASTERN AND CENTRAL UNITED STATES AND CANADA, William M. Harlow. Best one-volume guide to 140 trees. Full descriptions, woodlore, range, etc. Over 600 illustrations. Handy size. 288pp. 4½ x 6⅜. 0-486-20395-6

GROWING AND USING HERBS AND SPICES, Milo Miloradovich. Versatile handbook provides all the information needed for cultivation and use of all the herbs and spices available in North America. 4 illustrations. Index. Glossary. 236pp. 5⅜ x 8½.
0-486-25058-X

BIG BOOK OF MAZES AND LABYRINTHS, Walter Shepherd. 50 mazes and labyrinths in all–classical, solid, ripple, and more–in one great volume. Perfect inexpensive puzzler for clever youngsters. Full solutions. 112pp. 8⅛ x 11. 0-486-22951-3

PIANO TUNING, J. Cree Fischer. Clearest, best book for beginner, amateur. Simple repairs, raising dropped notes, tuning by easy method of flattened fifths. No previous skills needed. 4 illustrations. 201pp. 5⅜ x 8½. 0-486-23267-0

MAGIC AND MYSTERY IN TIBET, Madame Alexandra David-Neel. Experiences among lamas, magicians, sages, sorcerers, Bonpa wizards. A true psychic discovery. 32 illustrations. 321pp. 5⅜ x 8½. (Available in U.S. only.)   0-486-22682-4

THE EGYPTIAN BOOK OF THE DEAD, E. A. Wallis Budge. Complete reproduction of Ani's papyrus, finest ever found. Full hieroglyphic text, interlinear transliteration, word-for-word translation, smooth translation. 533pp. 6½ x 9¼.

0-486-21866-X

HISTORIC COSTUME IN PICTURES, Braun & Schneider. Over 1,450 costumed figures in clearly detailed engravings–from dawn of civilization to end of 19th century. Captions. Many folk costumes. 256pp. 8⅜ x 11¾.   0-486-23150-X

MATHEMATICS FOR THE NONMATHEMATICIAN, Morris Kline. Detailed, college-level treatment of mathematics in cultural and historical context, with numerous exercises. Recommended Reading Lists. Tables. Numerous figures. 641pp. 5⅜ x 8½.

0-486-24823-2

PROBABILISTIC METHODS IN THE THEORY OF STRUCTURES, Isaac Elishakoff. Well-written introduction covers the elements of the theory of probability from two or more random variables, the reliability of such multivariable structures, the theory of random function, Monte Carlo methods of treating problems incapable of exact solution, and more. Examples. 502pp. 5⅜ x 8½.   0-486-40691-1

THE RIME OF THE ANCIENT MARINER, Gustave Doré, S. T. Coleridge. Doré's finest work; 34 plates capture moods, subtleties of poem. Flawless full-size reproductions printed on facing pages with authoritative text of poem. "Beautiful. Simply beautiful."–*Publisher's Weekly*. 77pp. 9¼ x 12.   0-486-22305-1

SCULPTURE: Principles and Practice, Louis Slobodkin. Step-by-step approach to clay, plaster, metals, stone; classical and modern. 253 drawings, photos. 255pp. 8⅛ x 11.

0-486-22960-2

THE INFLUENCE OF SEA POWER UPON HISTORY, 1660–1783, A. T. Mahan. Influential classic of naval history and tactics still used as text in war colleges. First paperback edition. 4 maps. 24 battle plans. 640pp. 5⅜ x 8½.   0-486-25509-3

THE STORY OF THE TITANIC AS TOLD BY ITS SURVIVORS, Jack Winocour (ed.). What it was really like. Panic, despair, shocking inefficiency, and a little heroism. More thrilling than any fictional account. 26 illustrations. 320pp. 5⅜ x 8½.

0-486-20610-6

ONE TWO THREE . . . INFINITY: Facts and Speculations of Science, George Gamow. Great physicist's fascinating, readable overview of contemporary science: number theory, relativity, fourth dimension, entropy, genes, atomic structure, much more. 128 illustrations. Index. 352pp. 5⅜ x 8½.   0-486-25664-2

DALÍ ON MODERN ART: The Cuckolds of Antiquated Modern Art, Salvador Dalí. Influential painter skewers modern art and its practitioners. Outrageous evaluations of Picasso, Cézanne, Turner, more. 15 renderings of paintings discussed. 44 calligraphic decorations by Dalí. 96pp. 5⅜ x 8½. (Available in U.S. only.)   0-486-29220-7

ANTIQUE PLAYING CARDS: A Pictorial History, Henry René D'Allemagne. Over 900 elaborate, decorative images from rare playing cards (14th–20th centuries): Bacchus, death, dancing dogs, hunting scenes, royal coats of arms, players cheating, much more. 96pp. 9¼ x 12¼.   0-486-29265-7

LIGHT AND SHADE: A Classic Approach to Three-Dimensional Drawing, Mrs. Mary P. Merrifield. Handy reference clearly demonstrates principles of light and shade by revealing effects of common daylight, sunshine, and candle or artificial light on geometrical solids. 13 plates. 64pp. 5⅜ x 8½. 0-486-44143-1

ASTROLOGY AND ASTRONOMY: A Pictorial Archive of Signs and Symbols, Ernst and Johanna Lehner. Treasure trove of stories, lore, and myth, accompanied by more than 300 rare illustrations of planets, the Milky Way, signs of the zodiac, comets, meteors, and other astronomical phenomena. 192pp. 8⅜ x 11. 0-486-43981-X

JEWELRY MAKING: Techniques for Metal, Tim McCreight. Easy-to-follow instructions and carefully executed illustrations describe tools and techniques, use of gems and enamels, wire inlay, casting, and other topics. 72 line illustrations and diagrams. 176pp. 8¼ x 10⅞. 0-486-44043-5

MAKING BIRDHOUSES: Easy and Advanced Projects, Gladstone Califf. Easy-to-follow instructions include diagrams for everything from a one-room house for bluebirds to a forty-two-room structure for purple martins. 56 plates; 4 figures. 80pp. 8¾ x 6⅜. 0-486-44183-0

LITTLE BOOK OF LOG CABINS: How to Build and Furnish Them, William S. Wicks. Handy how-to manual, with instructions and illustrations for building cabins in the Adirondack style, fireplaces, stairways, furniture, beamed ceilings, and more. 102 line drawings. 96pp. 8¾ x 6⅜. 0-486-44259-4

THE SEASONS OF AMERICA PAST, Eric Sloane. From "sugaring time" and strawberry picking to Indian summer and fall harvest, a whole year's activities described in charming prose and enhanced with 79 of the author's own illustrations. 160pp. 8¼ x 11. 0-486-44220-9

THE METROPOLIS OF TOMORROW, Hugh Ferriss. Generous, prophetic vision of the metropolis of the future, as perceived in 1929. Powerful illustrations of towering structures, wide avenues, and rooftop parks–all features in many of today's modern cities. 59 illustrations. 144pp. 8¼ x 11. 0-486-43727-2

THE PATH TO ROME, Hilaire Belloc. This 1902 memoir abounds in lively vignettes from a vanished time, recounting a pilgrimage on foot across the Alps and Apennines in order to "see all Europe which the Christian Faith has saved." 77 of the author's original line drawings complement his sparkling prose. 272pp. 5⅜ x 8½. 0-486-44001-X

THE HISTORY OF RASSELAS: Prince of Abissinia, Samuel Johnson. Distinguished English writer attacks eighteenth-century optimism and man's unrealistic estimates of what life has to offer. 112pp. 5⅜ x 8½. 0-486-44094-X

A VOYAGE TO ARCTURUS, David Lindsay. A brilliant flight of pure fancy, where wild creatures crowd the fantastic landscape and demented torturers dominate victims with their bizarre mental powers. 272pp. 5⅜ x 8½. 0-486-44198-9

Paperbound unless otherwise indicated. Available at your book dealer, online at **www.doverpublications.com**, or by writing to Dept. GI, Dover Publications, Inc., 31 East 2nd Street, Mineola, NY 11501. For current price information or for free catalogs (please indicate field of interest), write to Dover Publications or log on to **www.doverpublications.com** and see every Dover book in print. Dover publishes more than 500 books each year on science, elementary and advanced mathematics, biology, music, art, literary history, social sciences, and other areas.